Dice Activi
Mathematica ...g

Fluency • Understanding • Engagement

Mary Saltus and Chet Delani

Printed in the United States of America.

This book is printed on recycled paper.

Order Number 211096
ISBN 978-1-58324-326-8

F G H I J 20 19 18 17 16

395 Main Street
Rowley, MA 01969
www.didax.com

Dice Activities for Mathematical Thinking

Foreword

Successful math students manipulate numbers mentally. The activities in *Dice Activities for Mathematical Thinking* were created by teachers to engage students in developing fluency with the mathematical concepts of square numbers, square roots, prime numbers, factorials, summation, and integers. The activities are designed to empower students with the ability to address mathematical problems and challenges with a sense of curiosity and confidence.

These activities focus on the NCTM standards of Number and Operations and Algebra. They also address the standards of Reasoning, Problem Solving, and Probability. The NCTM standards are the framework of all published mathematics programs and state and local curricula frameworks; thus, these activities are easily integrated into a scope and sequence whenever the topic is addressed. In many instances the teacher will want to replace the activity in the school-based text with those found in this book, as they are challenging, more apt to provide long-term mastery, and develop a profound interest and curiosity about math.

The authors currently use *Dice Activities for Mathematical Thinking* as part of their curriculum to train elementary school teachers in how to teach mathematics. The activities require only the use of dice, a commonly available manipulative. They are easily adapted to home schooling and for parents who wish to participate in the mathematics education of their children. They provide an opportunity for students to play with big mathematic ideas without paper-and-pencil drill. The activities are engaging, generate a friendly competition, and provide immediate use of and reason for learning these mathematic concepts.

Our work is continually expanding, and we welcome any suggestions for modification of these activities that will lead to greater mathematical thinking on the part of our students. Submit any suggestions to: mathofcourse@gmail.com.

Contents

Authors' Introduction

Too often teachers are under pressure to get through the curriculum, which is often determined by chapters in the adopted text programs, driven by pacing charts, and measured by district-imposed assessment instruments. The purpose of chapter tests is to ensure that all teachers are not only using the same program but are essentially on the same page. "Research based" is often the mantra for system adoption of programs and practices, but who is looking at what is happening to the students' mathematical knowledge base? While test scores may improve or at least remain stable, students quickly forget what they don't understand. Short-term memory serves well for passing the frequent tests, but unless students have a firm grip on the content and concepts, it all falls away and must be retaught annually. Teachers in subsequent years wonder why the students don't know what is expected of them. Certainly the human mind is capable of learning more efficiently. The problem must lie in how math is taught, and therefore learned, and not in a malfunction of the students' capabilities.

So how does this particular book address these issues? It is important to acknowledge the value of these dice activities for students and how they impact their mathematical competence. The most powerful tool that needs to be developed in the mathematical journey is each student's mathematical thinking skills. If a student develops the disposition towards thinking mathematically, employs a curiosity of about why, and wonders how, then the student is on the road to independent thinking and a constructivist approach to problem solving. Rather than depending on memorized procedures, the student will actually think through the problem and develop a rationale for solution.

Fluency with number and operation is a critical skill for the journey into more complex mathematical challenges. Like basal texts, the activities in this book (and series) provide students with ample opportunity to practice basic skills and facts. The difference is that the dice activities are highly engaging, employing game theory as the motivating force to keep students focused.

The preceding book in the series stressed multiplication facts; *Dice Activities for Mathematical Thinking* emphasizes more sophisticated mathematical concepts such as prime and composite numbers, factorials, summation, square roots, and square numbers. These mathematical concepts are key elements of many algebraic patterns, and square numbers appear on a frequent basis. Students therefore need a working knowledge and quick recognition of these numbers. The activities in this book provide that knowledge base, helping students develop a fluency in working with a level of number that is more mathematical than arithmetic.

Factorials and summations surface in many of the problems that abound in assessment and instructional programs. A facility in working with these numbers and the ability to use them to strategize and to solve problems is invaluable. Students can function at various levels of problem solving in approaching factorial and summation-related challenges. Consider the problem of summation 4, noted as $\sum 4$. When asked to solve $\sum 4$, students should expand it to read: $\sum 4 = 4 + 3 + 2 + 1 = 10$. Depending on their mathematical competency, a variety of strategies will be employed. Some students will just begin to add the numbers as in the following: $4 + 3 = 7$, $7 + 2 = 9$, and $9 + 1 = 10$.

Other students might consider that they just recently found the solution to $\sum 3$ (= 6) and since $\sum 4$ includes $\sum 3 + 4$, then the answer merely requires them to add $6 + 4$, which equals 10. Some students will look for patterns to add sequences of numbers and strategize that the summation of even numbers might be an algebraic pattern of [.5*n*] x *n* + [.5*n*] ... in this case, half of 4 = 2, times 4 = 8, plus half of 4 = 10. The critical issue is that whatever strategy a student employs makes sense to that student and is not merely a repetition of the teacher-taught strategy. Students are more apt to remember their own solutions or at least be able to reconstruct them. Herein lies the power of differentiated instruction. Students need to be allowed to employ their own strategies to solve problems. This constructivist approach is the foundation of the major mathematical programs used in this country and the underpinnings of the state assessment instruments—the latter witnessed by the aspect of the test that requires students to explain their thinking and strategies.

This is not to imply that there are not multitudes of ways a teacher can differentiate learning within a lesson. Take, for example, an activity with prime numbers. For more mathematically competent students, a teacher may have students use a limited number of dice, say 4, to make equations that equal as many prime numbers as possible. For students who have not yet developed a fluency with number or mathematical thinking, the same problem can be posed in the same lesson while using 6 dice instead. And even more powerful, rather than the teacher assigning the use of 4 dice to some and 6 dice to others, the option can be left to the students. Students can operate at their own level of success and gradually move to more challenging possibilities as their level of confidence increases.

It should be noted that most of the activities in this book are designed for two teams of two students competing against each other. The team approach allows students to check their thinking and share strategies with their partner. In cases, however, where the more assertive partner does all the thinking and the less assertive partner willingly lets him/her take the lead, it is better to have one student play against another, since it requires both students to think, strategize, and make decisions. Having students play one-on-one is also a good assessment tool, as the teacher can more closely monitor individual progress. Whether playing individually or as a member of a team, students benefit from working with a shoulder partner when introduced to these activities.

Many of these activities can be explored on a larger scale. Take, for instance, the classic problem of using four 4s to write the numbers 1 to 100. This could be done as a whole-class activity, challenging the students to collaborate on solutions. A dramatic challenge would be for several classrooms at the same grade level to compete with one another. As the students closed in on all the solutions, they would discover that certain numbers are much more difficult and would employ the use of factorials, squaring numbers, and/or summation. Initially it might seem impossible to square any of the numbers, since only 4s can be used. Inserting a 4 into a square root symbol produces the number 2, which allows students to square numbers.

The joy of mathematical thinking is an experience that all children deserve, regardless of their mathematical ability. In a nutshell, that should be the kernel of the No Child Left Behind legislation. All children deserve and need a mathematical education that allows them to think and not merely memorize. But at the same time, it is folly to assume that all children have the same intellectual capacity and to legislate on the basis of that assumption. The educators of this country need to stand firm as to what our children deserve and what it means to be truly educated mathematically.

—Mary Saltus and Chet Delani

Meeting the NCTM Standards

NCTM STANDARDS Grades 5–8	*Dice Graph Activities* Pages 1–13	*Table Completion Chart Activities* Pages 15–24	*Four in a Row Activities* Pages 25–36	*Square Off Activities* Pages 37–48	*Cross Over Activities* Pages 49–60	*Tic-Tac-Toe Activities* Pages 61–83	*Aim For Activities* Pages 85–91	*Independent Explorations* Pages 93–118
Number and Operations								
Place value								
Equivalent representations	✗	✗	✗	✗	✗	✗	✗	✗
Positive and negative integers	✗	✗	✗	✗	✗	✗	✗	✗
Fractions, decimals, and percents								
Ratios and proportions								
Exponential notation	✗	✗	✗	✗	✗	✗	✗	✗
Factors, multiples, prime factorization	✗	✗	✗	✗	✗	✗	✗	✗
Compare quantities using integers							✗	
Relationships between operations	✗	✗	✗	✗	✗	✗	✗	✗
Properties of operations	✗	✗	✗	✗	✗	✗	✗	✗
Squaring and square roots	✗	✗	✗	✗	✗	✗	✗	✗
Fluency with operations	✗	✗	✗	✗	✗	✗	✗	✗
Select appropriate methods	✗	✗	✗	✗	✗	✗	✗	✗
Develop and analyze algorithms							✗	✗
Estimation	✗	✗	✗	✗	✗	✗	✗	✗
Algebra								
Generalize numeric patterns		✗						✗
Use algebraic symbols	✗	✗	✗	✗	✗	✗	✗	✗
Model situations with equations	✗	✗						✗
Data Analysis and Probability								
Represent and analyze data	✗	✗						
Predict outcomes	✗	✗	✗	✗	✗	✗		
Problem Solving	✗	✗	✗	✗	✗	✗	✗	✗
Reasoning and Proof	✗	✗	✗	✗	✗	✗	✗	✗
Communication		✗	✗	✗	✗	✗	✗	✗

Concepts

Square Numbers

- Toss a die. Square the number on the die.
- That is, multiply the number by itself. The product of the numbers is a square number.

  $3 \times 3 =$ **9** $\quad 5 \times 5 =$ **25** $\quad 4 \times 4 =$ **16**
- Toss 2 dice. Square the sum of the two numbers.
- That is, multiply the sum by itself. The product is a square number.

  $3 + 5 = 8$, then square the sum: $8 \times 8 =$ **64**

Closest Square Number

- Toss 2 red dice and find the sum. Toss 2 green dice and find the sum.
- Find the product of the two sums.
- What is the square number closest to this product?

  $5 + 4 = 9 \quad 6 + 2 = 8 \quad 9 \times 8 =$ **72**
- What square number is closest to 72? Is it 64, or is it 81?

  64 is the square number closest to **72**.

Square Root

- Toss a die. The number tossed is the square root of what number?
- That is, if you multiply the number by itself, What is the product?

  $\sqrt{1} \quad \sqrt{4} \quad \sqrt{9} \quad \sqrt{16} \quad \sqrt{25} \quad \sqrt{36}$

  Toss 7. $7 \times 7 =$ **$\sqrt{49}$**
- Toss 2 dice and find the sum. The sum is the square root of what number?
- That is, if you multiply the sum by itself, what is the product?

  $\sqrt{4} \quad \sqrt{9} \quad \sqrt{16} \quad \sqrt{25} \quad \sqrt{36}$
  $\sqrt{49} \quad \sqrt{64} \quad \sqrt{81} \quad \sqrt{100} \quad \sqrt{121}$
  $\sqrt{144}$

  Toss 3 and 8. $3 + 8 = 11$, and **11** = **$\sqrt{121}$**.

Prime Numbers – Numbers with exactly 2 factors: one and the number itself

- Toss 2 dice. Find the product. Add one to the product.
- Is this number prime?
- Toss 2 dice. Find the product. Either add 1 or subtract 1 from the product.
- Is this number prime?

Factorials – The sign for a factorial is an exclamation point (!)

- Toss a die. Find the factorial of the tossed number—that is, the **product** of all the numbers from 1, including the number tossed.

  $5! = 1 \times 2 \times 3 \times 4 \times 5 = 120$

Summation – The sign for summation is Σ.

- Toss a die. Find the summation of the tossed number—that is, the sum of all the numbers from 1, including the number tossed.

  $\Sigma 6 = 6 + 5 + 4 + 3 + 2 + 1 = 21$
- Toss two dice. Find the sum. Find the summation of the sum— that is, the sum of all the numbers from 1, including the sum of the tossed dice.

  $3 + 4 = 7$

  $\Sigma 7 = 7 + 6 + 5 + 4 + 3 + 2 + 1 = 28$

Positive and Negative Integers

- Green die = positive integer
- Red die = negative integer
- Toss a green die and a red die. Add the integers:

  $(+5) + (-6) = -1$

Square Number Chart – 1 to 144

1	2	3	4	5	6	7	8	9	10
11	12	13	14	15	16	17	18	19	20
21	22	23	24	25	26	27	28	29	30
31	32	33	34	35	36	37	38	39	40
41	42	43	44	45	46	47	48	49	50
51	52	53	54	55	56	57	58	59	60
61	62	63	64	65	66	67	68	69	70
71	72	73	74	75	76	77	78	79	80
81	82	83	84	85	86	87	88	89	90
91	92	93	94	95	96	97	98	99	100
101	102	103	104	105	106	107	108	109	110
111	112	113	114	115	116	117	118	119	120
121	122	123	124	125	126	127	128	129	130
131	132	133	134	135	136	137	138	139	140
141	142	143	144	145	146	147	148	149	150

Prime Number Chart – 1 to 100

1	2	3	4	5	6	7	8	9	10
11	12	13	14	15	16	17	18	19	20
21	22	23	24	25	26	27	28	29	30
31	32	33	34	35	36	37	38	39	40
41	42	43	44	45	46	47	48	49	50
51	52	53	54	55	56	57	58	59	60
61	62	63	64	65	66	67	68	69	70
71	72	73	74	75	76	77	78	79	80
81	82	83	84	85	86	87	88	89	90
91	92	93	94	95	96	97	98	99	100

Die/Dice Graph Activities

Contents

Directions for Die/Dice Graph Activities

Objectives

Develop a working knowledge of the mathematical concepts of

- Square numbers
- Square roots
- Prime numbers
- Positive/negative integers
- Factorials
- Summations
- Positive and negative integers

The graphs are an introductory lesson to familiarize students with the concepts. The simplicity of the activity makes it a tool for diversifying learning. Students may work individually or in teams of two. Some students may find it beneficial to stay with this activity, developing recognition and fluency, while others are ready for more challenging involvement.

Introduce the Die/Dice Graphs by demonstrating on an overhead.

How to Play

- Toss 1 die or 2 dice, depending on the activity.
- Perform the computation – operations differ for each activity.
- Solutions are shown on the bottom row of the graph.
- Find the solution and write it in the box above it, or write the number sentence that produced it. For example, for 16, write 4^2 or 4×4.
- See how many boxes can be filled in 25 tosses.

Suggestion

If students are struggling with determining the closest square number or prime number, suggest that they refer to the Square Number Chart or Prime Number Chart on pages viii–ix.

Variations

- The first team to fill a column is the winner.
- The first team that fills a column stops the activity. Teams use calculators to find the sums of all the numbers entered on the graph to determine the highest score.
- Toss the dice 10 times. The team with the highest sum wins. Keep records of tosses and use as a probability lesson.
- The team tosses the die or dice and does the computation. Instead of recording the solution, the teacher instructs the students to perform another calculation, such as:
  - Double or triple the solution
  - Halve the solution
  - Add 5 to the solution and halve the result
  - Add 7, 8, 9, 10, or 11 to the solution
  - Subtract 7, 8, 9, 10, or 11 (may result in a negative number)

After 5, 10, or 15 tosses, tally the answers to see which team has the highest or lowest score.

Square One Die Graph

How to Play

1. *Toss a die.*
2. *Square the number (multiply the number by itself—for example,* 3×3*)*
3. *Fill in the box above the square number with the equation (for example,* 3×3*, or the exponent* 3^2*).*
4. *How many boxes can you fill in 25 tosses?*

1	**4**	**9**	**16**	**25**	**36**

Square Sum of Two Dice Graph

How to Play

1. *Toss two dice. Find the sum.*
2. *Square the sum (multiply the sum by itself—for example, 7×7).*
3. *Fill in the box above the square number with the expression (for example, 7×7, or the exponent 7^2).*
4. *How many boxes can you fill in 25 tosses?*

1	**4**	**9**	**16**	**25**	**36**	**49**	**64**	**81**	**100**	**121**	**144**

Closest Square Number Graph

How to Play

1. *Toss 2 red dice. Find the sum.*
2. *Toss 2 green dice. Find the sum.*
3. *Multiply the sum of the red dice by the sum of the green dice.*
4. *Fill in the box above the square number that is closest to the product. (Example: red dice = 5 + 2 = 7, green dice = 4 + 4 = 8, 8 × 7 = 56; 56 is near both 49 and 64 but closer to 49; 49 is the closest square number. Write 56 in the box above 49.)*
5. *How many boxes can you fill in 25 tosses?*

1	**4**	**9**	**16**	**25**	**36**	**49**	**64**	**81**	**100**	**121**	**144**

One-Die Square Root Graph

How to Play

1. *Toss the die.*
2. *The tossed number is the solution to which square root expression on the chart?*
3. *Fill in the box above the square root expression with the square root. (For example, in the box above $\sqrt{4}$, write "2.")*
4. *How many boxes can you fill in 25 tosses?*

$\sqrt{1}$	$\sqrt{4}$	$\sqrt{9}$	$\sqrt{16}$	$\sqrt{25}$	$\sqrt{36}$

Two-Dice Square Root Graph

How to Play

1. *Toss two dice. Find the sum.*
2. *The sum of the two dice is the solution to which square root expression on the chart?*
3. *Fill in the box above the square root expression with the square root. (For example, in the box above $\sqrt{4}$, write "2.")*
4. *How many boxes can you fill in 25 tosses?*

$\sqrt{4}$	$\sqrt{9}$	$\sqrt{16}$	$\sqrt{25}$	$\sqrt{36}$	$\sqrt{49}$	$\sqrt{64}$	$\sqrt{81}$	$\sqrt{100}$	$\sqrt{121}$	$\sqrt{144}$

Prime Number

Die × Die + 1 Graph

How to Play

1. *Toss two dice. Find the product. Add one to the product.*
2. *If the product plus one equals a prime number, find the prime number on the graph.*
3. *Fill in the box above the prime number.*
4. *How many boxes can you fill in 25 tosses?*

2	**3**	**5**	**7**	**11**	**13**	**17**	**19**	**23**	**29**	**31**	**37**

Prime Number

Die × Die + or –1 Graph

How to Play

1. Toss two dice. Find the product.

2. Add one to the product. If it equals a prime number, fill in a box above the prime.

3. Subtract one from the product. If it equals a prime number, fill in a box above the prime.

4. How many boxes can you fill in 25 tosses?

2	**3**	**5**	**7**	**11**	**13**	**17**	**19**	**23**	**29**	**31**	**37**

One-Die Factorial (!) Graph

How to Play

1. *Toss a die.*
2. *In the box above the factorial of the number tossed, write the number tossed and the factorial symbol (!). The ! is the product of the number tossed and the entire sequence of natural numbers preceding that number. (For example, toss a 3. 3! = 3 x 2 x 1 = 6. In the box above 6, write 3!.)*
3. *How many boxes can you fill in 25 tosses?*

Here are the factorials for the numbers 1–6:

1! = 1	*2! = 2 × 1*	*3! =3 × 2 × 1*
4! = 4 × 3 × 2 × 1	*5! =5 × 4 × 3 × 2 × 1*	*6! = 6 × 5 × 4 × 3 × 2 × 1*

1	**2**	**6**	**24**	**120**	**720**

One-Die Summation (Σ) Graph

How to Play

1. *Toss a die.*
2. *Find the summation (Σ) of the number tossed. The* ***summation*** *is the sum of the number tossed and all the natural numbers preceding that number. (For example, toss a 4. Σ4 = 4 + 3 + 2 + 1 = 10.)*
3. *Fill in the box above the summation (for example, 10) with the mathematical symbol for summation (Σ) and the number tossed (in this example, Σ4).*
4. *How many boxes can you fill in 25 tosses?*

1	**3**	**6**	**10**	**15**	**21**

Two-Dice Summation (Σ) Graph

How to Play

1. *Toss two dice. Find the sum.*
2. *Find the summation of the sum tossed. The* ***summation (Σ)*** *is the sum tossed added to the sum of the sequence of natural numbers preceding that number. For example,* ***Σ9 = 9 + 8 + 7 + 6 + 5 + 4 + 3 + 2 + 1 = 45.***
3. *Fill in the box above the summation (Σ) of the sum with the summation sign and the sum. (For example, the sum of the two dice is 9; the summation of 9 is 45; above 45, write* ***Σ9****.)*
4. *How many boxes can you fill in 25 tosses?*

3	**6**	**10**	**15**	**21**	**28**	**36**	**45**	**55**	**66**	**78**

Positive/Negative Numbers Dice Graph

+ −

How to Play

Green die = positive number. Red die = negative number.

1. Toss a green die and a red die. Find the sum or difference.

__Example:__ green die = 3, red die = 5. Compute: (+3) + (–5) = –2.

2. Fill in a box above the answer to the dice toss.

3. How many boxes can you fill in 25 tosses?

–5	–4	–3	–2	–1	0	+1	+2	+3	+4	+5

Table Completion Activities

Contents

Directions for Table Completion Chart Activities

Objectives

Develop a working knowledge of the mathematical concepts of

- Square numbers
- Square roots
- Prime numbers
- Positive/negative integers
- Factorials
- Summations
- Positive and negative integers

Introduce the Table Completion Charts by demonstrating on an overhead and playing against the class. Two teams with 2 students on a team are suggested. Teams give students an opportunity to discuss moves and strategies and provide a check on correct computation.

How to Play

- Each team tosses a die. The higher number goes first.
- Team tosses a die or dice and performs the necessary computation. Operations differ for each activity.
- Team finds the solution and records it in the appropriate box on the chart.
- If the number has already been played, the team loses a turn.
- If a team records the wrong number, they erase it and lose a turn.
- The first team to complete their chart wins.

Suggestions

- Before placing a token on the chart, team members explain how they arrived at a solution:

For example:

Seven squared equals 7 × 7 = 49

5! = 5 × 4 × 3 × 2 × 1 = 120

- If students are struggling with determining the closest square number or prime number, suggest they refer to the Square Number Chart or Prime Number Chart on pages viii–ix.

Variations

Teams toss a die or dice and perform the required computation. Instead of recording the solution, teams perform any of the following variations and record the new solution next to the appropriate number.

- Double or triple the solution
- Halve the solution
- Add 5 to the solution and halve the result
- Add 7, 8, 9, 10, or 11 to the solution
- Subtract 7, 8, 9, 10, or 11 from the solution (may result in a negative number)
- Tally both columns in the activity and see if there is a pattern

After 5, 10, or 15 tosses, teams tally the answers to see which team has the higher score.

Discussion

- Is this a game of luck or skill?

Square the Die Table Completion

- Each team tosses a die.
- Higher number goes first.

How to Play

1. Toss a die. Square the number (multiple the number by itself—for example, 3 x 3).

2. Record the solution in the appropriate box (for example, if 3 is tossed, write $3^2 = 9$ in the box next to it).

3. If the number has already been tossed, lose a turn.

4. If the team records the wrong number, they erase it and lose a turn.

5. The first team to complete their table wins.

Team: ____________________

Die Tossed	Square the Number
6	
5	
4	
3	
2	
1	

Team: ____________________

Die Tossed	Square the Number
6	
5	
4	
3	
2	
1	

- Each team tosses a die.
- Higher number goes first.

Square Two Dice Table Completion

How to Play

1. *Toss 2 dice. Find the sum. Square the sum (multiply the sum by itself—for example, 7 × 7).*
2. *Record the square of the sum next to the sum in the table. (For example, for 7 × 7, write $7^2 = 49$.)*
3. *If the sum has already been tossed, lose a turn.*
4. *If the team records the wrong number, they erase it and lose a turn.*
5. *The first team to complete their table wins.*

Team: ____________________

Sum	Square the Sum
12	
11	
10	
9	
8	
7	
6	
5	
4	
3	
2	

Team: ____________________

Sum	Square the Sum
12	
11	
10	
9	
8	
7	
6	
5	
4	
3	
2	

Closest Square Number

Table Completion

How to Play

1. Each team tosses a die. Higher number goes first.

2. Toss 2 red dice and find the sum. Toss 2 green dice and find the sum.

2. Multiply the sum of the red dice by the sum of the green dice.

3. Record the product next to the closest square number in the table.

4. If the square number already has a product recorded next to it, team loses a turn. If the team records the wrong number, they erase it and lose a turn.

6. The first team to complete their table wins.

Team: ____________________

Square Number	Product of Sums
144	
121	
100	
81	
64	
49	
36	
25	
16	
9	
4	

Team: ____________________

Square Number	Product of Sums
144	
121	
100	
81	
64	
49	
36	
25	
16	
9	
4	

One-Die Square Root Table Completion

- Each team tosses a die.
- Higher number goes first.

How to Play

1. *Toss a die. The tossed number is the solution to which square root expression? Look for it in the table.*
2. *Record the square root next to the square root expression in the table.*
3. *If the square root has already been tossed, lose a turn.*
4. *If a team records the wrong number, they erase it and lose a turn.*
5. *The first team to complete their table wins.*

Team: ______________________

Square Root Expression	Square Root
$\sqrt{36}$	
$\sqrt{25}$	
$\sqrt{16}$	
$\sqrt{9}$	
$\sqrt{4}$	
$\sqrt{1}$	

Team: ______________________

Square Root Expression	Square Root
$\sqrt{36}$	
$\sqrt{25}$	
$\sqrt{16}$	
$\sqrt{9}$	
$\sqrt{4}$	
$\sqrt{1}$	

Two-Dice Square Root Table Completion

How to Play

- Each team tosses a die.
- Higher number goes first.

1. Toss 2 dice. Find the sum. The sum is the solution to which square root expression? Look for it in the table.

2. Record the square root next to the square root expression in the table.

3. If the square root has already been tossed, lose a turn.

4. If a team records the wrong number, they erase it and lose a turn.

5. The first team to complete their table wins.

Team: ______________________

Square Root Expression	Square Root
$\sqrt{144}$	
$\sqrt{121}$	
$\sqrt{100}$	
$\sqrt{81}$	
$\sqrt{64}$	
$\sqrt{49}$	
$\sqrt{36}$	
$\sqrt{25}$	
$\sqrt{16}$	
$\sqrt{9}$	
$\sqrt{4}$	

Team: ______________________

Square Root Expression	Square Root
$\sqrt{144}$	
$\sqrt{121}$	
$\sqrt{100}$	
$\sqrt{81}$	
$\sqrt{64}$	
$\sqrt{49}$	
$\sqrt{36}$	
$\sqrt{25}$	
$\sqrt{16}$	
$\sqrt{9}$	
$\sqrt{4}$	

One-Die Factorial (!) Table Completion

- Each team tosses a die.
- Higher number goes first.

How to Play

1. Toss a die.

2. Record the ***factorial (!)*** *in the table next to the number tossed.*

3. If the number has already been tossed, lose a turn.

4. If a team records the wrong factorial, they erase it and lose a turn.

5. The first team to complete their table wins.

$1! = 1$ $2! = 2 \times 1$ $3! = 3 \times 2 \times 1$

$4! = 4 \times 3 \times 2 \times 1$ $5! = 5 \times 4 \times 3 \times 2 \times 1$ $6! = 6 \times 5 \times 4 \times 3 \times 2 \times 1$

Team: ______________________

Die Tossed	!
6	
5	
4	
3	
2	
1	

Team: ______________________

Die Tossed	!
6	
5	
4	
3	
2	
1	

One-Die Summation (Σ) Table Completion

- Each team tosses a die.
- Higher number goes first.

How to Play

1. *Toss a die.*
2. *Record the* **summation (Σ)** *in the table next to the number tossed.*
3. *If the number has already been tossed, lose a turn.*
4. *If a team records the wrong summation, they erase it and lose a turn.*
5. *The first team to complete their table wins.*

$\Sigma 1 = 1$ $\Sigma 2 = 2 + 1$ $\Sigma 3 = 3 + 2 + 1$

$\Sigma 4 = 4 + 3 + 2 + 1$ $\Sigma 5 = 5 + 4 + 3 + 2 + 1$ $\Sigma 6 = 6 + 5 + 4 + 3 + 2 + 1$

Team: ____________________

Die Tossed	Σ
6	
5	
4	
3	
2	
1	

Team: ____________________

Die Tossed	Σ
6	
5	
4	
3	
2	
1	

Two-Dice Summation (Σ) Table Completion

- Each team tosses a die.
- Higher number goes first.

How to Play

1. *Toss 2 dice. Find the sum.*
2. *Record the* ***summation (Σ)*** *of the sum next to the sum in the table.*
3. *If the sum has already been tossed, lose a turn.*
4. *If a team records the wrong number, they erase it and lose a turn.*
5. *The first team to complete their table wins.*

Team: ______________________

Sum Tossed	Σ
12	
11	
10	
9	
8	
7	
6	
5	
4	
3	
2	

Team: ______________________

Sum Tossed	Σ
12	
11	
10	
9	
8	
7	
6	
5	
4	
3	
2	

Four in a Row Activities

Contents

Directions for Four in a Row Activities

Objectives

- Develop a working knowledge of the mathematical concepts of:
  - Square numbers
  - Square roots
  - Prime numbers
  - Factorials
  - Summations
  - Positive and negative integers
- Develop an awareness of an opponent's possible moves.
- Analyze an opponent's possible moves in order to develop a blocking strategy.
- Identify the role of luck versus skill in an activity using dice.
- Develop communication and cooperation skills by working in teams of two students.

Introduce the **Four in a Row** activities by demonstrating on an overhead and playing against the class. Two teams with two students on a team are suggested. Teams give students an opportunity to discuss moves and strategies and provide a check on correct computation.

How to Play

- Teams toss die or dice, depending on the activity, and perform the required computation—operations differ for each activity. For example:

  In the square root activities, if the sum of the two dice tossed is 7, then players look for the number for which 7 is the square root.
  In the factorial activities, if the sum of the two dice tossed is 5, then players look for 5!, or 120 (5! = 5 x 4 x 3 x 2 x 1 = 120).
- Teams attempt to line up four tokens vertically, horizontally, or diagonally before the opposing team does.
- The first team to align four tokens in a row wins.

Suggestions

- Before placing a token on the chart, team members explain how they arrived at a solution.
- If students are struggling with determining the closest square number or prime number, suggest that they refer to the Square Number Chart and Prime Number Chart on pages viii–ix.

Discussion

- This activity is similar to the games *Othello* and *Pente*, where defense is important. How does the toss of the dice influence strategy? Is this activity more a game of defense or offense?
- Does this activity involve more luck or skill?
- Keep a recording of each dice toss. Which combinations were tossed the most? The least?

Four in a Row

Square the Die Chart

- Each team tosses a die.
- Higher number goes first.
- Each team chooses a color token.

How to Play

1. *Toss a die. Square the number (multiply the number by itself—for example, 7 × 7).*
2. *Place a token on the square number.*
3. *The first team to get 4 tokens in a row, vertically, horizontally, or diagonally, wins.*

36	1	16	25	9	4	16
25	9	36	1	4	16	1
1	16	4	9	25	26	4
4	25	9	16	36	1	25
9	36	1	4	16	25	9
16	4	25	36	1	9	36
25	9	16	1	36	4	25

Four in a Row

Square Two Dice Chart

- Each team tosses a die.
- Higher number goes first.
- Each team chooses a color token.

How to Play

1. *Toss 2 dice. Find the sum. Square the sum (multiply the sum by itself—for example, 7 × 7).*
2. *Place a token on the square number.*
3. *The first team to get 4 tokens in a row, vertically, horizontally, or diagonally, wins.*

36	121	9	25	81	16	4
49	64	144	100	36	25	81
25	49	36	64	4	81	64
64	36	81	49	121	16	49
100	25	4	16	36	49	144
16	81	121	49	100	9	64
9	36	64	144	49	25	100

Four in a Row

Closest Square Number Chart

- Each team tosses a die.
- Higher number goes first.
- Each team chooses a color token.

How to Play

1. *Toss 2 red dice and find the sum. Toss 2 green dice and find the sum.*
2. *Multiply the sum of the red dice by the sum of the green dice.*

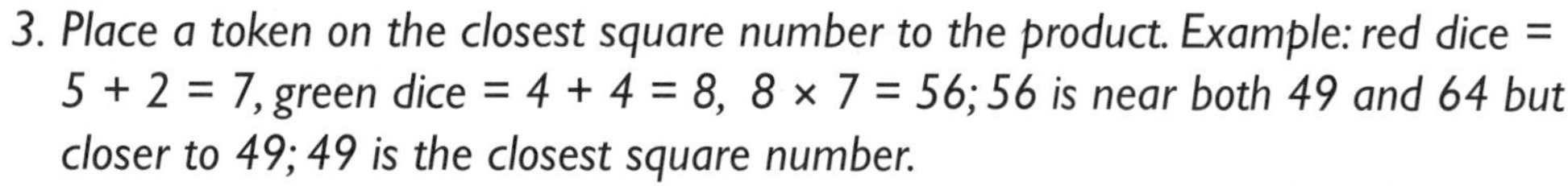

3. *Place a token on the closest square number to the product. Example: red dice = 5 + 2 = 7, green dice = 4 + 4 = 8, 8 × 7 = 56; 56 is near both 49 and 64 but closer to 49; 49 is the closest square number.*

4. *First team to get 4 tokens in a row, vertically, horizontally, or diagonally, wins.*

36	121	9	25	81	16	4
49	64	144	100	36	25	81
25	49	36	64	4	81	64
64	36	81	49	121	16	49
100	25	4	16	36	49	144
16	81	121	49	100	9	64
9	36	64	144	49	25	100

- Each team tosses a die.
- Higher number goes first.
- Each team chooses a color token.

Four in a Row

One-Die Square Root Chart

How to Play

1. Toss a die. The number tossed is the solution to which square root expression on the chart?

2. Place a token on that expression.

3. The first team to get 4 tokens in a row, vertically, horizontally, or diagonally, wins.

$\sqrt{36}$	$\sqrt{1}$	$\sqrt{16}$	$\sqrt{25}$	$\sqrt{9}$	$\sqrt{4}$	$\sqrt{16}$
$\sqrt{25}$	$\sqrt{9}$	$\sqrt{36}$	$\sqrt{1}$	$\sqrt{4}$	$\sqrt{16}$	$\sqrt{1}$
$\sqrt{1}$	$\sqrt{16}$	$\sqrt{4}$	$\sqrt{9}$	$\sqrt{25}$	$\sqrt{26}$	$\sqrt{4}$
$\sqrt{4}$	$\sqrt{25}$	$\sqrt{9}$	$\sqrt{16}$	$\sqrt{36}$	$\sqrt{1}$	$\sqrt{25}$
$\sqrt{9}$	$\sqrt{36}$	$\sqrt{1}$	$\sqrt{4}$	$\sqrt{16}$	$\sqrt{25}$	$\sqrt{9}$
$\sqrt{16}$	$\sqrt{4}$	$\sqrt{25}$	$\sqrt{36}$	$\sqrt{1}$	$\sqrt{9}$	$\sqrt{36}$
$\sqrt{25}$	$\sqrt{9}$	$\sqrt{16}$	$\sqrt{1}$	$\sqrt{36}$	$\sqrt{4}$	$\sqrt{25}$

Four in a Row

Two-Dice Square Root Chart

- Each team tosses a die.
- Higher number goes first.
- Each team chooses a color token.

How to Play

1. Toss 2 dice. Find the sum. The sum is the solution to which square root expression on the chart?

2. Place a token on that expression.

3. The first team to get 4 tokens in a row, vertically, horizontally, or diagonally, wins.

$\sqrt{36}$	$\sqrt{121}$	$\sqrt{9}$	$\sqrt{25}$	$\sqrt{81}$	$\sqrt{16}$	$\sqrt{4}$
$\sqrt{49}$	$\sqrt{64}$	$\sqrt{144}$	$\sqrt{100}$	$\sqrt{36}$	$\sqrt{25}$	$\sqrt{81}$
$\sqrt{25}$	$\sqrt{49}$	$\sqrt{36}$	$\sqrt{64}$	$\sqrt{4}$	$\sqrt{81}$	$\sqrt{64}$
$\sqrt{64}$	$\sqrt{36}$	$\sqrt{81}$	$\sqrt{49}$	$\sqrt{121}$	$\sqrt{16}$	$\sqrt{49}$
$\sqrt{100}$	$\sqrt{25}$	$\sqrt{4}$	$\sqrt{16}$	$\sqrt{36}$	$\sqrt{49}$	$\sqrt{144}$
$\sqrt{16}$	$\sqrt{81}$	$\sqrt{121}$	$\sqrt{49}$	$\sqrt{100}$	$\sqrt{9}$	$\sqrt{64}$
$\sqrt{9}$	$\sqrt{36}$	$\sqrt{64}$	$\sqrt{144}$	$\sqrt{49}$	$\sqrt{25}$	$\sqrt{100}$

Four in a Row

Die × Die + or –1 Prime Number Chart

- Each team tosses a die.
- Higher number goes first.
- Each team chooses a color token.

How to Play

1. *Toss 2 dice. Find the product.*
2. *Either add 1 to or subtract 1 from the product.*
3. *If that number is prime, place a token on the number.*
4. *If the number is not prime, or the prime number has a token on it, lose a turn.*
5. *The first team to get 4 tokens in a row, vertically, horizontally, or diagonally, wins.*

31	2	17	13	7	5	23
5	19	7	5	11	31	7
7	11	3	19	5	11	23
11	13	7	5	13	2	11
13	5	11	17	7	29	3
29	11	3	13	7	11	5
37	7	11	23	13	5	19

Four in a Row One-Die Factorial (!) Chart

- Each team tosses a die.
- Higher number goes first.
- Each team chooses a color token.

$1! = 1$

$2! = 2 \times 1$

$3! = 3 \times 2 \times 1$

$4! = 4 \times 3 \times 2 \times 1$

$5! = 5 \times 4 \times 3 \times 2 \times 1$

$6! = 6 \times 5 \times 4 \times 3 \times 2 \times 1$

How to Play

1. Toss a die.

2. Place a token on the factorial of the number tossed.

3. First team to get 4 tokens in a row, vertically, horizontally, or diagonally, wins.

720	1	24	120	6	2	24
120	6	720	1	2	24	1
1	24	2	6	120	720	2
2	120	6	24	720	1	120
6	720	1	2	24	120	6
24	2	120	720	1	6	720
120	6	24	1	720	2	120

Four in a Row

One-Die Summation (Σ) Chart

- Each team tosses a die.
- Higher number goes first.
- Each team chooses a color token.

How to Play

1. *Toss a die. Place a token on the* ***summation (Σ)*** *of the number tossed.*
   $\sum 1 = 1$ $\sum 2 = 2 + 1$ $\sum 3 = 3 + 2 + 1$
   $\sum 4 = 4 + 3 + 2 + 1$ $\sum 5 = 5 + 4 + 3 + 2 + 1$ $\sum 6 = 6 + 5 + 4 + 3 + 2 + 1$
2. *The first team to get 4 tokens in a row, vertically, horizontally, or diagonally, wins.*

21	1	10	15	6	3	10
15	6	21	1	3	10	1
1	10	3	6	15	21	3
3	15	6	10	21	1	15
6	21	1	3	10	15	6
10	3	15	21	1	6	21
15	6	10	1	21	3	15

- Each team tosses a die.
- Higher number goes first.
- Each team chooses a color token.

Four in a Row

Two-Dice Summation (Σ) Chart

How to Play

1. *Toss two dice. Find the sum of the two dice.*
2. *Place a token on the* ***summation (Σ)*** *of the sum. Example:* $\sum 3 = 3 + 2 + 1 = 6$.
3. *First team to get 4 tokens in a row, vertically, horizontally, or diagonally, wins.*

21	66	6	15	45	10	3
28	36	78	55	21	15	45
15	28	21	36	3	45	36
36	21	45	28	66	10	28
55	15	3	10	21	28	78
10	45	66	28	55	6	36
6	21	36	78	28	15	55

Four in a Row

Positive and Negative Numbers Chart

- Each team tosses a die.
- Higher number goes first.
- Each team chooses a color token.

Green die = positive number
Red die = negative number

How to Play

1. Toss a green die and a red die. Compute the sum or difference.
Example: green die = 3, red die = 5. Compute: (+3) + (–5) = –2.

2. Place a token on the positive or negative integer.

3. The first team to get 4 tokens in a row, vertically, horizontally, or diagonally, wins.

+3	–4	+1	+4	–1	–3	+2
–3	–1	–2	0	+1	+5	–4
–5	0	+2	–1	+2	–2	+3
+4	+1	0	–2	–3	–1	0
–1	+4	–2	+3	–4	0	+5
0	+2	+1	–3	0	+3	–1
+1	–5	–2	0	+2	–4	+1

Square Off Activities

Contents

Directions for Square Off Activities

Objectives

- Develop a working knowledge of the mathematical concepts of:
  - Square numbers
  - Square roots
  - Prime numbers
  - Factorials
  - Summations
  - Positive and negative integers
- Develop an awareness of an opponent's possible moves.
- Analyze an opponent's possible moves in order to develop a blocking strategy.
- Identify the role of luck versus skill in an activity using dice.
- Develop communication and cooperation skills by working in teams of two students.

Introduce the **Square Off** activities by demonstrating on an overhead and playing against the class. Two teams with two students on a team are suggested. Teams give students an opportunity to discuss moves and strategies and provide a check on correct computation.

How to Play

- Each team tosses a die. The higher number goes first.
- Teams toss die or dice and perform the required computation—operations differ for each activity.
- Teams attempt to arrange four tokens to form any size square, 2-by-2, 3-by-3, 4-by-4, and so on. Orientation of the square can be on the diagonal.
- The first team to form three squares wins.

Suggestions

- Before placing a token on the chart, team members explain how they arrived at a solution:

  Examples:

  Seven squared equals 7 × 7 = 49

  5! = 5 × 4 × 3 × 2 × 1 = 120
- If students are struggling with determining the closest square number or prime number, suggest that they refer to the Square Number Chart and Prime Number Chart on page viii–ix.

Discussion

- Is this more a game of luck or skill?
- Is there more opportunity in **Square Off** than in **Four in a Row** or **Cross Over** to play defensively—that is, to prevent the opposing team from forming a square?
- Which of the three activities—**Square Off**, **Four in a Row**, or **Cross Over**—offers more opportunities to block the other team? Why is that?
- What math or strategies have you and your team partner learned from each other?
- Would you prefer to play these games with a partner or without? Why?

- Each team tosses a die.
- Higher number goes first.
- Each team chooses a color token.

Square Off

Square the Die Chart

How to Play

1. *Toss a die. Square the number (multiply the number by itself—for example, 3 x 3).*
2. *Place a token on the square number.*
3. *Teams attempt to place tokens to form a square. Squares can be 2-by-2, 3-by-3, 4-by-4, and so on. Orientation of the square can be on the diagonal.*
4. *First team to place tokens forming three squares wins.*

36	1	16	25	9	4	16
25	9	36	1	4	16	1
1	16	4	9	25	36	4
4	25	9	16	36	1	25
9	36	1	4	16	25	9
16	4	25	36	1	9	36
25	9	16	1	36	4	25

- Each team tosses a die.
- Higher number goes first.
- Each team chooses a color token.

Square Off

Square Two Dice Chart

How to Play

1. *Toss 2 dice. Find the sum. Square the sum (multiply the sum by itself—for example, 7 × 7).*
2. *Place a token on the square number.*
3. *Teams attempt to place tokens to form a square. Squares can be 2-by-2, 3-by-3, 4-by-4, and so on. Orientation of the square can be on the diagonal.*
4. *The first team to place tokens forming three squares wins.*

36	121	9	25	81	16	4
49	64	144	100	36	25	81
25	49	36	64	4	81	64
64	36	81	49	121	16	49
100	25	4	16	36	49	144
16	81	121	49	100	9	64
9	36	64	144	49	25	100

Square Off

Closest Square Number Chart

- Each team tosses a die.
- Higher number goes first.
- Each team chooses a color token.

How to Play

1. Toss 2 red dice and find the sum. Toss 2 green dice and find the sum.

2. Multiply the sum of the red dice by the sum of the green dice.

3. Place a token on the square number closest to the product.

4. Teams attempt to place tokens to form a square. Squares can be 2-by-2, 3-by-3, 4-by-4, and so on. Orientation of the square can be on the diagonal.

5. First team to place tokens forming three squares wins.

36	121	9	25	81	16	4
49	64	144	100	36	25	81
25	49	36	64	4	81	64
64	36	81	49	121	16	49
100	25	4	16	36	49	144
16	81	121	49	100	9	64
9	36	64	144	49	25	100

Square Off

One-Die Square Root Chart

- Each team tosses a die.
- Higher number goes first.
- Each team chooses a color token.

How to Play

1. *Toss a die. The tossed number is the solution to which square root expression? Find it on the chart.*
2. *Place a token on that expression.*
3. *Teams attempt to place tokens to form a square. Squares can be 2-by-2, 3-by-3, 4-by-4, and so on. Orientation of the square can be on the diagonal.*
4. *The first team to place tokens forming three squares wins.*

$\sqrt{36}$	$\sqrt{1}$	$\sqrt{16}$	$\sqrt{25}$	$\sqrt{9}$	$\sqrt{4}$	$\sqrt{16}$
$\sqrt{25}$	$\sqrt{9}$	$\sqrt{36}$	$\sqrt{1}$	$\sqrt{4}$	$\sqrt{16}$	$\sqrt{1}$
$\sqrt{1}$	$\sqrt{16}$	$\sqrt{4}$	$\sqrt{9}$	$\sqrt{25}$	$\sqrt{36}$	$\sqrt{4}$
$\sqrt{4}$	$\sqrt{25}$	$\sqrt{9}$	$\sqrt{16}$	$\sqrt{36}$	$\sqrt{1}$	$\sqrt{25}$
$\sqrt{9}$	$\sqrt{36}$	$\sqrt{1}$	$\sqrt{4}$	$\sqrt{16}$	$\sqrt{25}$	$\sqrt{9}$
$\sqrt{16}$	$\sqrt{4}$	$\sqrt{25}$	$\sqrt{36}$	$\sqrt{1}$	$\sqrt{9}$	$\sqrt{36}$
$\sqrt{25}$	$\sqrt{9}$	$\sqrt{16}$	$\sqrt{1}$	$\sqrt{36}$	$\sqrt{4}$	$\sqrt{25}$

- Each team tosses a die.
- Higher number goes first.
- Each team chooses a color token.

How to Play

Square Off
Two-Dice Square Root Chart

1. Toss two dice. Find the sum. The sum is the solution to which square root expression? Find it on the chart.

2. Place a token on that expression.

3. Teams attempt to place tokens to form a square. Squares can be 2-by-2, 3-by-3, 4-by-4, and so on. Orientation of the square can be on the diagonal.

4. The first team to place tokens forming three squares wins.

$\sqrt{36}$	$\sqrt{121}$	$\sqrt{9}$	$\sqrt{25}$	$\sqrt{81}$	$\sqrt{16}$	$\sqrt{4}$
$\sqrt{49}$	$\sqrt{64}$	$\sqrt{144}$	$\sqrt{100}$	$\sqrt{36}$	$\sqrt{25}$	$\sqrt{81}$
$\sqrt{25}$	$\sqrt{49}$	$\sqrt{36}$	$\sqrt{64}$	$\sqrt{4}$	$\sqrt{81}$	$\sqrt{64}$
$\sqrt{64}$	$\sqrt{36}$	$\sqrt{81}$	$\sqrt{49}$	$\sqrt{121}$	$\sqrt{16}$	$\sqrt{49}$
$\sqrt{100}$	$\sqrt{25}$	$\sqrt{4}$	$\sqrt{16}$	$\sqrt{36}$	$\sqrt{49}$	$\sqrt{144}$
$\sqrt{16}$	$\sqrt{81}$	$\sqrt{121}$	$\sqrt{49}$	$\sqrt{100}$	$\sqrt{9}$	$\sqrt{64}$
$\sqrt{9}$	$\sqrt{36}$	$\sqrt{64}$	$\sqrt{144}$	$\sqrt{49}$	$\sqrt{25}$	$\sqrt{100}$

Square Off

Die × Die + or −1 Prime Number Chart

- Each team tosses a die.
- Higher number goes first.
- Each team chooses a color token.

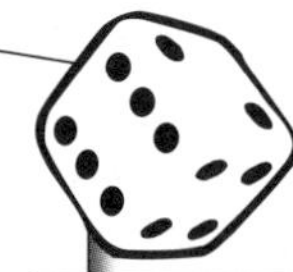

How to Play

1. *Toss 2 dice. Find the product. Either add 1 to the product or subtract 1 from the product.*
2. *If the number you get is a prime number, place a token on that number.*
3. *If the number is not prime, or the prime number has a token on it, lose a turn.*
4. *Teams attempt to place tokens to form a square. Squares can be 2-by-2, 3-by-3, 4-by-4, and so on. Orientation of the square can be on the diagonal.*
5. *The first team to place tokens forming three squares wins.*

31	2	17	13	7	5	23
5	19	7	5	11	31	7
7	11	3	19	5	11	23
11	13	7	5	13	2	11
13	5	11	17	7	29	3
29	11	3	13	7	11	5
37	7	11	23	13	5	19

Square Off One-Die Factorial (!) Chart

- Each team tosses a die.
- Higher number goes first.
- Each team chooses a color token.

1! = 1
2! = 2 × 1
3! = 3 × 2 × 1
4! = 4 × 3 × 2 × 1
5! = 5 × 4 × 3 × 2 × 1
6! = 6 × 5 × 4 × 3 × 2 × 1

How to Play

1. *Toss a die.*
2. *Place a token on the factorial of the number tossed.*
3. *Teams attempt to place tokens to form a square. Squares can be 2-by-2, 3-by-3, 4-by-4, and so on. Orientation of the square can be on the diagonal.*
4. *The first team to place tokens forming 3 squares wins.*

720	1	24	120	6	2	24
120	6	720	1	2	24	1
1	24	2	6	120	720	2
2	120	6	24	720	1	120
6	720	1	2	24	120	6
24	2	120	720	1	6	720
120	6	24	1	720	2	120

Square Off

One-Die Summation (∑) Chart

- Each team tosses a die.
- Higher number goes first.
- Each team chooses a color token.

How to Play

*1. Toss a die. Place a token on the **summation (∑)** of the number tossed.*

$\sum 1 = 1$ $\sum 2 = 2 + 1$ $\sum 3 = 3 + 2 + 1$

$\sum 4 = 4 + 3 + 2 + 1$ $\sum 5 = 5 + 4 + 3 + 2 + 1$ $\sum 6 = 6 + 5 + 4 + 3 + 2 + 1$

2. Teams attempt to place tokens to form a square. Squares can be 2-by-2, 3-by-3, 4-by-4, and so on. Orientation of the square can be on the diagonal.

3. The first team to place tokens forming three squares wins.

21	1	10	15	6	3	10
15	6	21	1	3	10	1
1	10	3	6	15	21	3
3	15	6	10	21	1	15
6	21	1	3	10	15	6
10	3	15	21	1	6	21
15	6	10	1	21	3	15

Square Off

Two-Dice Summation (Σ) Chart

- Each team tosses a die.
- Higher number goes first.
- Each team chooses a color token.

How to Play

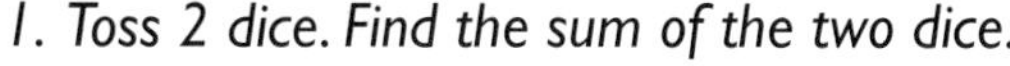

1. Toss 2 dice. Find the sum of the two dice.

2. Place a token on the **summation (Σ)** *of the sum. Example:*

Σ9 = 9 + 8 + 7 + 6 + 5 + 4 + 3 + 2 + 1.

3. Teams attempt to place tokens to form a square. Squares can be 2-by-2, 3-by-3, 4-by-4, and so on. Orientation of the square can be on the diagonal.

4. The first team to place tokens forming three squares wins.

21	66	6	15	45	10	3
28	36	78	55	21	15	45
15	28	21	36	3	45	36
36	21	45	28	66	10	28
55	15	3	10	21	28	78
10	45	66	28	55	6	36
6	21	36	78	28	15	55

Square Off

Positive and Negative Numbers Chart

Green die = positive number.

Red die = negative number.

- Each team tosses a die.
- Higher number goes first.
- Each team chooses a color token.

How to Play

1. Toss a green die and a red die. Compute the sum or difference.

Example: green die = 3, red die = 5. Compute: (+3) + (–5) = –2.

2. Place a token on the positive or negative number.

3. If the number has a token on it, lose a turn.

4. Teams attempt to place tokens to form a square.

5. The first team to place tokens forming three squares wins.

+3	–4	+1	+4	–1	–3	+2
–3	–1	–2	0	+1	+5	–4
–5	0	+2	–1	+2	–2	+3
+4	+1	0	–2	–3	–1	0
–1	+4	–2	+3	–4	0	+5
0	+2	+1	–3	0	+3	–1
+1	–5	–2	0	+2	–4	+1

Cross Over Activities

Contents

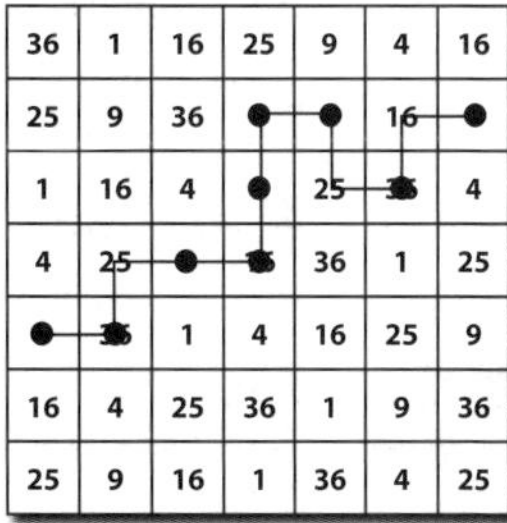

36	1	16	25	9	4	16
25	9	36	●	●	16	●
1	16	4	●	25	36	4
4	25	●	36	36	1	25
●	36	1	4	16	25	9
16	4	25	36	1	9	36
25	9	16	1	36	4	25

Directions for Cross Over Activities

Objectives

- Develop a working knowledge of the mathematical concepts of:
  - Square numbers
  - Square roots
  - Prime numbers
  - Factorials
  - Summations
  - Positive and negative integers
- Analyze an opponent's possible moves in order to develop a blocking strategy.
- Identify the role of luck versus skill in an activity using dice.
- Develop communication and cooperation skills by working in teams of two students.
- Provide an opportunity for reflection and self-correction through teamwork.

Introduce the **Cross Over Activities** by demonstrating on an overhead and playing against the class. Two teams with two students on a team are suggested. Teams give students an opportunity to discuss moves and strategies and provide a check on correct computation.

How to Play

- Each team tosses a die. The higher number goes first.
- Team A tosses a die or dice and performs the required computation. Operations differ for each activity.
- Team A places a token on the solution on the chart.
- With each toss of the die or dice, the teams attempt to place their tokens so they form a continuous path zigzagging vertically, horizontally, or diagonally from space to adjacent space from one side of the chart to the other.
- If a number is taken, the team loses the turn.
- The first team to form a continuous path connecting both sides wins.

Suggestions

- Before placing a token on the chart, team members explain how they arrived at a solution. For example: "5 factorial (!) equals 5 × 4 × 3 × 2 × 1, which equals 120."
- If students are struggling with determining the closest square or prime number, suggest that they refer to the Square Number Chart or Prime Number Chart on pages viii–ix.

Variation

- Both teams start play in either the outside right or outside left column of the chart. If no box in either column contains the solution to the team's first die toss, the team loses its turn.

Discussion

- Is this more a game of luck or skill?
- Which of the three activities—**Square Off, Four in a Row,** or **Cross Over**—offers more opportunities to block the other team? Why?

Cross Over Square the Die Chart

- Each team tosses a die.
- Higher number goes first.
- Each team chooses a color token.

How to Play

1. Toss a die. Square the number (multiply the number by itself—for example, 3 × 3).

2. Place a token on that square number anywhere on the chart. With each turn, place tokens so they form a continuous path—zigzagging horizontally, diagonally, or vertically—from one side of the chart to the other.

3. If a number is taken, lose a turn.

4. First team to "cross over" wins.

36	1	16	25	9	4	16
25	9	36	●	●	16	●
1	16	4	●	25	●	4
4	25	●	●	36	1	25
●	●	1	4	16	25	9
16	4	25	36	1	9	36
25	9	16	1	36	4	25

36	1	16	25	9	4	16
25	9	36	1	4	16	1
1	16	4	9	25	36	4
4	25	9	16	36	1	25
9	36	1	4	16	25	9
16	4	25	36	1	9	36
25	9	16	1	36	4	25

Cross Over Square Two Dice Chart

- Each team tosses a die.
- Higher number goes first.
- Each team chooses a color token.

How to Play

1. *Toss two dice. Find the sum and square it (multiply the sum by itself—for example, 7 × 7).*
2. *Place a token on that square number anywhere on the chart. With each turn, place tokens so they form a continuous path—zigzagging horizontally, diagonally, or vertically—from one side of the chart to the other.*
3. *If a number is taken, lose a turn.*
4. *First team to "cross over" wins.*

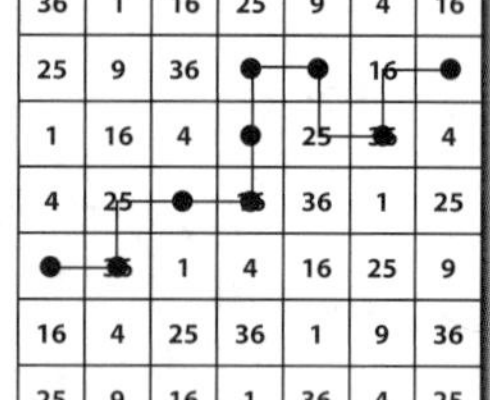

36	1	16	25	9	4	16
25	9	36			16	
1	16	4		25	36	4
4	25		16	36	1	25
	36	1	4	16	25	9
16	4	25	36	1	9	36
25	9	16	1	36	4	25

36	121	9	25	81	16	4
49	64	144	100	36	25	81
25	49	36	64	4	81	64
64	36	81	49	121	16	49
100	25	4	16	36	49	144
16	81	121	49	100	9	64
9	36	64	144	49	25	100

Cross Over

Closest Square Number Chart

- Each team tosses a die.
- Higher number goes first.
- Each team chooses a color token.

36	1	16	25	9	4	16
25	9	36			16	
1	16	4		25		4
4	25			36	1	25
		1	4	16	25	9
16	4	25	36	1	9	36
25	9	16	1	36	4	25

How to Play

1. Toss 2 red dice and find the sum. Toss 2 green dice and find the sum.

2. Multiply the sum of the red dice by the sum of the green dice.

3. Place a token on the square number closest to the product.

4. Place a token on that square number anywhere on the chart. With each turn, place tokens so they form a continuous path—zigzagging horizontally, diagonally, or vertically—from one side of the chart to the other.

5. If a number is taken, lose a turn.

6. First team to "cross over" wins.

36	121	9	25	81	16	4
49	64	144	100	36	25	81
25	49	36	64	4	81	64
64	36	81	49	121	16	49
100	25	4	16	36	49	144
16	81	121	49	100	9	64
9	36	64	144	49	25	100

Cross Over

One-Die Square Root Chart

- Each team tosses a die.
- Higher number goes first.
- Each team chooses a color token.

How to Play

1. Toss a die. The tossed number is the solution to which square root expression?

2. Find that expression on the chart and place a token on it.

3. With each turn, try to place tokens so they form a continuous path—zigzagging horizontally, diagonally, or vertically—from one side of the chart to the other.

4. If a number is taken, lose a turn.

5. First team to "cross over" wins.

$\sqrt{36}$	$\sqrt{1}$	$\sqrt{16}$	$\sqrt{25}$	$\sqrt{9}$	$\sqrt{4}$	$\sqrt{16}$
$\sqrt{25}$	$\sqrt{9}$	$\sqrt{36}$	$\sqrt{1}$	$\sqrt{4}$	$\sqrt{16}$	$\sqrt{1}$
$\sqrt{1}$	$\sqrt{16}$	$\sqrt{4}$	$\sqrt{9}$	$\sqrt{25}$	$\sqrt{26}$	$\sqrt{4}$
$\sqrt{4}$	$\sqrt{25}$	$\sqrt{9}$	$\sqrt{16}$	$\sqrt{36}$	$\sqrt{1}$	$\sqrt{25}$
$\sqrt{9}$	$\sqrt{36}$	$\sqrt{1}$	$\sqrt{4}$	$\sqrt{16}$	$\sqrt{25}$	$\sqrt{9}$
$\sqrt{16}$	$\sqrt{4}$	$\sqrt{25}$	$\sqrt{36}$	$\sqrt{1}$	$\sqrt{9}$	$\sqrt{36}$
$\sqrt{25}$	$\sqrt{9}$	$\sqrt{16}$	$\sqrt{1}$	$\sqrt{36}$	$\sqrt{4}$	$\sqrt{25}$

Cross Over

Two-Dice Square Root Chart

- Each team tosses a die.
- Higher number goes first.
- Each team chooses a color token.

How to Play

1. Toss 2 dice. Find the sum.

2. The sum is the solution to which square root expression? Place a token on that expression.

3. With each turn, place tokens so they form a continuous path—zigzagging horizontally, diagonally, or vertically—from one side of the chart to the other.

4. If a number is taken, lose a turn.

5. First team to "cross over" wins.

$\sqrt{36}$	$\sqrt{121}$	$\sqrt{9}$	$\sqrt{25}$	$\sqrt{81}$	$\sqrt{16}$	$\sqrt{4}$
$\sqrt{49}$	$\sqrt{64}$	$\sqrt{144}$	$\sqrt{100}$	$\sqrt{36}$	$\sqrt{25}$	$\sqrt{81}$
$\sqrt{25}$	$\sqrt{49}$	$\sqrt{36}$	$\sqrt{64}$	$\sqrt{4}$	$\sqrt{81}$	$\sqrt{64}$
$\sqrt{64}$	$\sqrt{36}$	$\sqrt{81}$	$\sqrt{49}$	$\sqrt{121}$	$\sqrt{16}$	$\sqrt{49}$
$\sqrt{100}$	$\sqrt{25}$	$\sqrt{4}$	$\sqrt{16}$	$\sqrt{36}$	$\sqrt{49}$	$\sqrt{144}$
$\sqrt{16}$	$\sqrt{81}$	$\sqrt{121}$	$\sqrt{49}$	$\sqrt{100}$	$\sqrt{9}$	$\sqrt{64}$
$\sqrt{9}$	$\sqrt{36}$	$\sqrt{64}$	$\sqrt{144}$	$\sqrt{49}$	$\sqrt{25}$	$\sqrt{100}$

Cross Over

Die × Die + or –1 Prime Number Chart

- Each team tosses a die.
- Higher number goes first.
- Each team chooses a color token.

How to Play

1. *Toss 2 dice. Find the product. Either add 1 to or subtract 1 from the product.*
2. *If the resulting number is a prime number, place a token on that number. If the number is not a prime number, or the prime number has a token on it, lose a turn.*
3. *With each turn, place tokens so they form a continuous path—zigzagging horizontally, diagonally, or vertically—from one side of the chart to the other.*
4. *If a number is taken, lose a turn.*
5. *First team to "cross over" wins.*

31	2	17	13	7	5	23
5	19	7	5	11	31	7
7	11	3	19	5	11	23
11	13	7	5	13	2	11
13	5	11	17	7	29	3
29	11	3	13	7	11	5
37	7	11	23	13	5	19

Cross Over One-Die Factorial (!) Chart

- Each team tosses a die.
- Higher number goes first.
- Each team chooses a color token.

1! = 1

2! = 2 × 1

3! = 3 × 2 × 1

4! = 4 × 3 × 2 × 1

5! = 5 × 4 × 3 × 2 × 1

6! = 6 × 5 × 4 × 3 × 2 × 1

1. *Toss a die. Place a token on the* ***factorial (!)*** *of the number tossed.*
2. *With each turn, place tokens so they form a continuous path—zigzagging horizontally, diagonally, or vertically—from one side of the chart to the other.*
3. *If a number is taken, lose a turn.*
4. *First team to "cross over" wins.*

720	1	24	120	6	2	24
120	6	720	1	2	24	1
1	24	2	6	120	720	2
2	120	6	24	720	1	120
6	720	1	2	24	120	6
24	2	120	720	1	6	720
120	6	24	1	720	2	120

Cross Over

One-Die Summation (Σ) Chart

- Each team tosses a die.
- Higher number goes first.
- Each team chooses a color token.

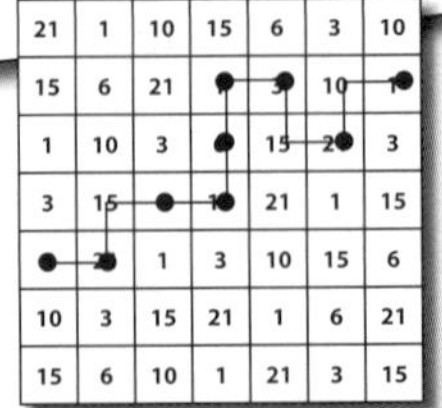

How to Play

1. *Toss a die. Place a token on the* **summation (Σ)** *of the number tossed.*

   $\sum 1 = 1$ $\sum 2 = 2 + 1$ $\sum 3 = 3 + 2 + 1$

   $\sum 4 = 4 + 3 + 2 + 1$ $\sum 5 = 5 + 4 + 3 + 2 + 1$ $\sum 6 = 6 + 5 + 4 + 3 + 2 + 1$
2. *With each turn, place tokens so they form a continuous path—zigzagging horizontally, diagonally, or vertically—from one side of the chart to the other.*
3. *If a number is taken, lose a turn.*
4. *First team to "cross over" wins.*

21	1	10	15	6	3	10
15	6	21	1	3	10	1
1	10	3	6	15	21	3
3	15	6	10	21	1	15
6	21	1	3	10	15	6
10	3	15	21	1	6	21
15	6	10	1	21	3	15

Cross Over

Two-Dice Summation (Σ) Chart

- Each team tosses a die.
- Higher number goes first.
- Each team chooses a color token.

How to Play

1. Toss 2 dice. Find the sum of the two dice.

2. Place a token on the **summation (Σ)** *of the sum. Example:*
Σ9 = 9 + 8 + 7 + 6 + 5 + 4 + 3 + 2 + 1.

3. With each turn, try to place tokens so they form a continuous path—zigzagging horizontally, diagonally, or vertically—from one side of the chart to the other.

4. If a number is taken, lose a turn.

5 First team to "cross over" wins.

21	66	6	15	45	10	3
28	36	78	55	21	15	45
15	28	21	36	3	45	36
36	21	45	28	66	10	28
55	15	3	10	21	28	78
10	45	66	28	55	6	36
6	21	36	78	28	15	55

Cross Over

Positive and Negative Numbers Chart

Green die = positive number.

Red die = negative number.

- Each team tosses a die.
- Higher number goes first.
- Each team chooses a color token.

How to Play

1. *Toss a green die and a red die. Compute the sum or difference. Example: green die = 3, red die = –5. Compute: (+3) + (–5) = –2.*
2. *Place a token on the positive or negative number.*
3. *With each turn, try to place tokens so they form a continuous path from one side of the chart to the other.*
4. *If a number is taken, lose a turn.*
5. *First team to "cross over" wins.*

+3	–4	+1	+4	–1	–3	+2
–3	–1	–2	0	+1	+5	–4
–5	0	+2	–1	+2	–2	+3
+4	+1	0	–2	–3	–1	0
–1	+4	–2	+3	–4	0	+5
0	+2	+1	–3	0	+3	–1
+1	–5	–2	0	+2	–4	+1

Tic-Tac-Toe/Four-Grid Tic-Tac-Toe Activities

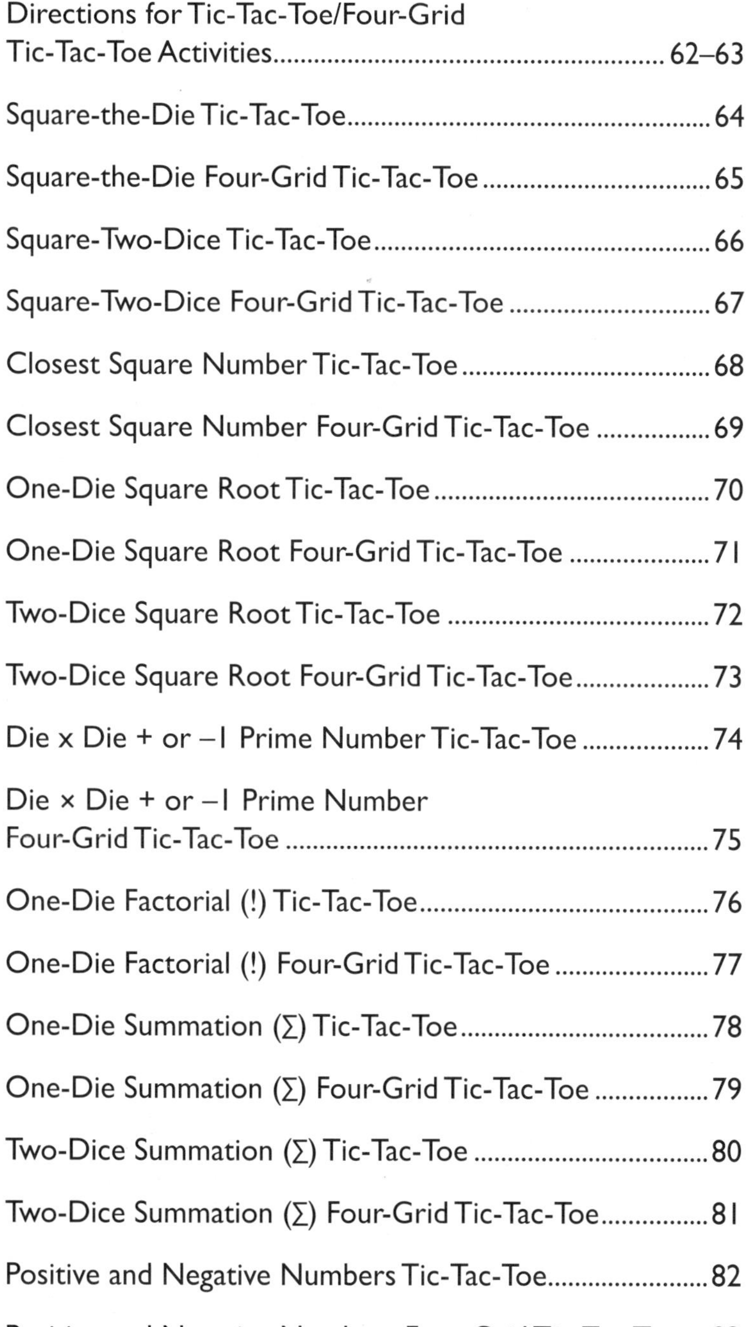

Contents

Directions for Tic-Tac-Toe/ Four-Grid Tic-Tac-Toe Activities

Objectives

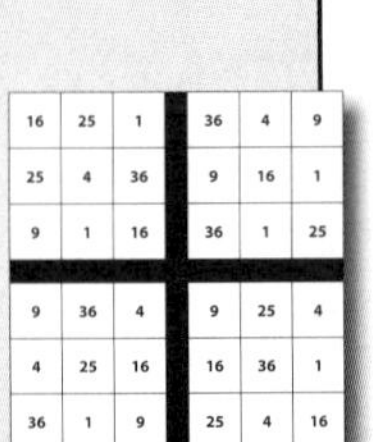

- Develop a working knowledge of the mathematical concepts of:
  - Square numbers
  - Square roots
  - Prime numbers
  - Factorials
  - Summations
  - Positive and negative integers
- Analyze an opponent's possible moves in order to develop a blocking strategy.
- Identify the role of luck versus skill in an activity using dice.
- Develop communication and cooperation skills by working in teams of two students.
- Provide an opportunity for reflection and self-correction through teamwork.

Tic-Tac-Toe is a familiar game form. These Tic-Tac-Toe activities provide a challenging and playful variation to use in mastering powerful and important math concepts.

The Tic-Tac-Toe activity is paired with a **Four-Grid Tic-Tac-Toe** activity providing a way to diversify while reinforcing specific mathematical concepts. This presents opportunities for students to practice playing **Tic-Tac-Toe** with each of the mathematical concepts before moving on to the more complicated **Four-Grid Tic-Tac-Toe**.

How to Play: Tic-Tac-Toe Activity

- Introduce the **Tic-Tac-Toe** activity by demonstrating on an overhead and playing against the class.
- Two teams with 2 students on a team are suggested. Teams give students an opportunity to discuss moves and strategies and provide a check on correct computation.
- Decide which team will use the X and which will use the O.
- Each team chooses a token and tosses a die. The higher number goes first.
- Teams toss a die or dice and perform the required computation. Operations differ for each activity.
- With each toss of the die or dice, the teams attempt to place their tokens in continuous alignment vertically, horizontally, or diagonally to win the game.
- If the solution is not shown on the grid or already has a token on it, the team loses a turn.
- The first team to form a Tic-Tac-Toe vertically, horizontally, or diagonally wins.
- The team winning 2 out of 3 games is the winner.

Suggestions

- Before placing a token on the chart, team members explain how they arrived at a solution. For example:

  "Seven squared is 7 × 7, which equals 49."

  "Five factorial (5!) is 1 × 2 × 3 × 4 × 5, or 120."
- If students are struggling with determining the closest square or prime number, suggest that they refer to the Square Number and Prime Number Charts on pages viii–ix.

Variations

- Teams place a token on every box where the solution appears.
- A team replaces the opposing team's token with their own.

Discussion

- Does the person who goes first have an advantage?
- Is this a game of luck or skill? Does the dice toss influence your strategy?
- Does the dice toss influence the outcome of the game?
- Is there a fair chance of each solution being tossed?

How to Play: Four-Grid Tic-Tac-Toe Activity

- Introduce the Four-Grid Tic-Tac-Toe activity by demonstrating on an overhead and playing against the class.
- Each team chooses a token and tosses a die. The higher number goes first.
- Teams toss a die or dice and perform the required computation. Operations differ for each activity.
- Teams locate the solution on any of the four Tic-Tac-Toe grids and place a token on only one of the solutions.
- With each toss of the die or dice, teams attempt to place their tokens in continuous alignment vertically, horizontally, or diagonally, forming as many Tic-Tac-Toe wins as possible.
- If the solution is not shown on any of the grids or already has a token on it, the team loses a turn.
- When no more plays are possible, the teams count their Tic-Tac-Toe wins. The team with the most Tic-Tac-Toes wins.

Variation

- Teams place a token on every box where the solution appears on all four Tic-Tac-Toe grids.
- Opposing teams agree to use the same strategy to see what happens.
- Opposing teams agree to each use a different strategy to see what happens.

Discussion

- What was your strategy in trying to win? Were you playing offensively or defensively? Did you play on one grid at a time, or did you try to play on all four grids simultaneously?
- Which strategy works best: trying to get the most three tokens in a row or trying to block your opponent?
- Discuss what would happen if both teams used the same strategy throughout the game.
- Discuss what might happen if opposing teams let each other know whether they would play offensively or defensively.

Square the Die Tic-Tac-Toe

- Each team tosses a die.
- Higher number goes first.
- Each team chooses a color token.

How to Play

1. *Toss a die.* ***Square*** *the number (multiply the number by itself—for example, 3 × 3).*
2. *Place a token on the square number.*
3. *If a number is taken, lose a turn.*
4. *The first team to get three tokens in a row wins the game.*
5. *Play 3 games. The team winning 2 out of 3 games wins.*

36	25	16
4	9	4
25	16	1

Square the Die

Four-Grid Tic-Tac-Toe

- Each team tosses a die.
- Higher number goes first.
- Each team chooses a color token.

How to Play

1. *Toss a die. Square the number (multiply the number by itself—for example, 3 × 3).*
2. *Find the square number on any of the Tic-Tac-Toe grids and place a token on it.*
3. *If the number is not available on any grid, lose a turn.*
4. *Team with the most "three tokens in a row" wins.*

16	25	1	36	4	9
25	4	36	9	16	1
9	1	16	36	1	25
9	36	4	9	25	4
4	25	16	16	36	1
36	1	9	25	4	16

Square Two Dice Tic-Tac-Toe

- Each team tosses a die.
- Higher number goes first.
- Each team chooses a color token.

How to Play

1. Toss 2 dice. Find the sum.

2. Square the sum (multiply the sum by itself—for example, 7 × 7).

3. Place a token on the square number.

4. If the number is taken, lose a turn.

5. The first team to get three tokens in a row wins the game.

6. Play 3 games. The team winning 2 out of 3 games wins.

36	**25**	**121**
64	**49**	**9**
100	**16**	**81**

Square Two Dice
Four-Grid Tic-Tac-Toe

- Each team tosses a die.
- Higher number goes first.
- Each team chooses a color token.

How to Play

1. *Toss 2 dice. Find the sum. Square the sum —for example, 7 × 7).*
2. *Find the square number on any of the Tic-Tac-Toe grids and place a token on it.*
3. *If the number is not available on any grid, lose a turn.*
4. *Team with the most "three tokens in a row" wins.*

49	36	64	100	64	121
100	25	16	25	49	81
81	36	9	16	64	36
16	81	9	121	49	25
36	64	144	100	36	49
49	25	49	64	81	4

Closest Square Number Tic-Tac-Toe

1. *Toss 2 red dice and find the sum. Toss 2 green dice and find the sum.*
2. *Multiply the sum of the red dice by the sum of the green dice.*
3. *Place a token on the square number closest to the product.*
4. *If the number is taken, lose a turn.*
5. *The first team to get three tokens in a row wins the game.*
6. *Play 3 games. The team winning 2 out of 3 games wins.*

How to Play

- Each team tosses a die.
- Higher number goes first.
- Each team chooses a color token.

36	**25**	**121**
64	**49**	**9**
100	**16**	**81**

Closest Square Number

Four-Grid Tic-Tac-Toe

- Each team tosses a die.
- Higher number goes first.
- Each team chooses a color token.

How to Play

1. Toss 2 red dice and find the sum. Toss 2 green dice and find the sum.

2. Multiply the sum of the red dice by the sum of the green dice.

3. Place a token on the square number closest to the product.

4. If the number is not available on any grid, lose a turn.

5. The team with the most "three tokens in a row" wins.

49	36	64	100	64	121
100	25	16	25	49	81
81	36	9	16	64	36
16	81	9	121	49	25
36	64	144	100	36	49
49	25	49	64	81	4

One-Die Square Root Tic-Tac-Toe

- Each team tosses a die.
- Higher number goes first.
- Each team chooses a color token.

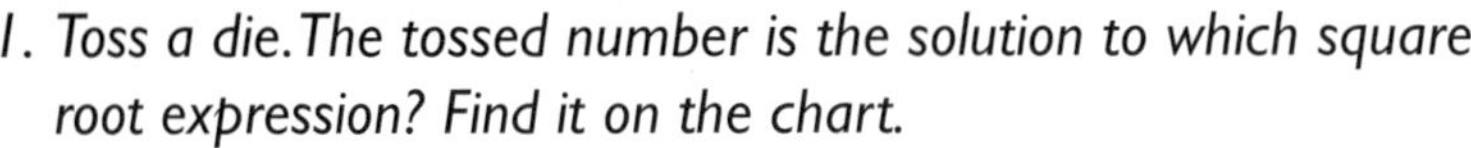

How to Play

1. *Toss a die. The tossed number is the solution to which square root expression? Find it on the chart.*
2. *Place a token on that expression.*
3. *If the expression is taken, lose a turn.*
4. *The first team to get three tokens in a row wins the game.*
5. *Play 3 games. The team winning 2 out of 3 games wins.*

$\sqrt{36}$	$\sqrt{25}$	$\sqrt{16}$
$\sqrt{4}$	$\sqrt{9}$	$\sqrt{4}$
$\sqrt{25}$	$\sqrt{16}$	$\sqrt{1}$

One-Die Square Root

Four-Grid Tic-Tac-Toe

- Each team tosses a die.
- Higher number goes first.
- Each team chooses a color token.

How to Play

1. Toss a die. The tossed number is the solution to which square root expression? Find it on one of the grids.

2. Place a token on that expression.

3. If the expression is not available on any grid, lose a turn.

4. Team with the most "three tokens in a row" wins.

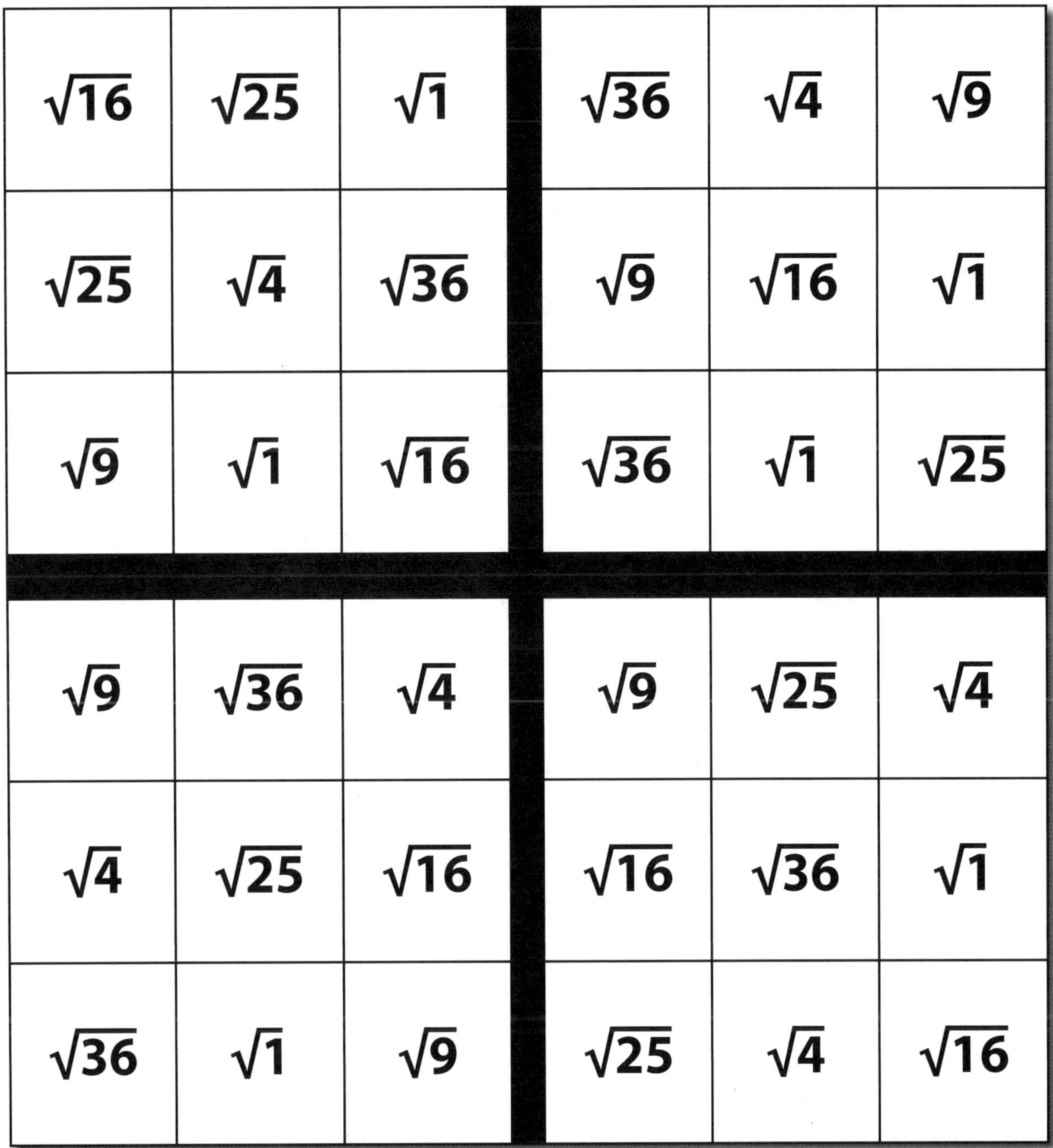

$\sqrt{16}$	$\sqrt{25}$	$\sqrt{1}$	$\sqrt{36}$	$\sqrt{4}$	$\sqrt{9}$
$\sqrt{25}$	$\sqrt{4}$	$\sqrt{36}$	$\sqrt{9}$	$\sqrt{16}$	$\sqrt{1}$
$\sqrt{9}$	$\sqrt{1}$	$\sqrt{16}$	$\sqrt{36}$	$\sqrt{1}$	$\sqrt{25}$
$\sqrt{9}$	$\sqrt{36}$	$\sqrt{4}$	$\sqrt{9}$	$\sqrt{25}$	$\sqrt{4}$
$\sqrt{4}$	$\sqrt{25}$	$\sqrt{16}$	$\sqrt{16}$	$\sqrt{36}$	$\sqrt{1}$
$\sqrt{36}$	$\sqrt{1}$	$\sqrt{9}$	$\sqrt{25}$	$\sqrt{4}$	$\sqrt{16}$

- Each team tosses a die.
- Higher number goes first.
- Each team chooses a color token.

Two-Dice Square Root Tic-Tac-Toe

How to Play

1. Toss the dice. Find the sum.

2. The sum is the solution to which square root expression? Find it on one of the grids.

3. Place a token on that expression.

4. If the square root expression is taken, lose a turn.

5. The first team to get three tokens in a row wins the game.

6. Play 3 games. The team winning 2 out of 3 games wins.

$\sqrt{36}$	$\sqrt{25}$	$\sqrt{121}$
$\sqrt{64}$	$\sqrt{49}$	$\sqrt{9}$
$\sqrt{100}$	$\sqrt{16}$	$\sqrt{81}$

Two-Dice Square Root

Four-Grid Tic-Tac-Toe

How to Play

- Each team tosses a die.
- Higher number goes first.
- Each team chooses a color token.

1. Toss the dice. Find the sum.

2. The sum is the solution to which square root expression? Find it on one of the grids.

3. Place a token on that expression.

4. If the square root expression is not available on any grid, lose a turn.

5. The team with the most "three tokens in a row" wins.

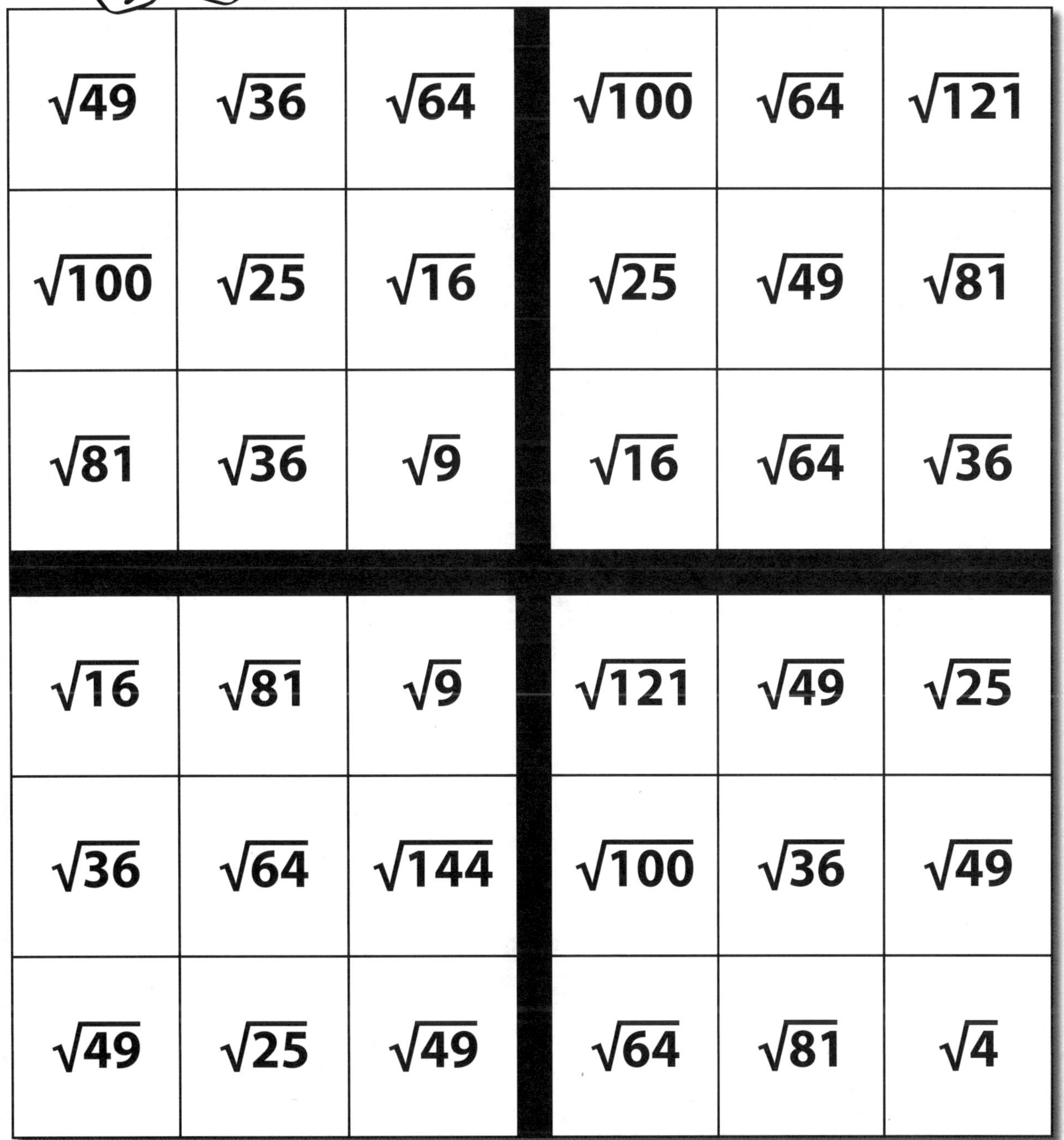

$\sqrt{49}$	$\sqrt{36}$	$\sqrt{64}$	$\sqrt{100}$	$\sqrt{64}$	$\sqrt{121}$
$\sqrt{100}$	$\sqrt{25}$	$\sqrt{16}$	$\sqrt{25}$	$\sqrt{49}$	$\sqrt{81}$
$\sqrt{81}$	$\sqrt{36}$	$\sqrt{9}$	$\sqrt{16}$	$\sqrt{64}$	$\sqrt{36}$
$\sqrt{16}$	$\sqrt{81}$	$\sqrt{9}$	$\sqrt{121}$	$\sqrt{49}$	$\sqrt{25}$
$\sqrt{36}$	$\sqrt{64}$	$\sqrt{144}$	$\sqrt{100}$	$\sqrt{36}$	$\sqrt{49}$
$\sqrt{49}$	$\sqrt{25}$	$\sqrt{49}$	$\sqrt{64}$	$\sqrt{81}$	$\sqrt{4}$

- Each team tosses a die.
- Higher number goes first.
- Each team chooses a color token.

Die × Die + or –1 Prime Number Tic-Tac-Toe

How to Play

1. Toss 2 dice. Find the product. Either add 1 to the product or subtract 1 from the product.
2. If that number is a prime number, place a token on the number.
3. If the number is not prime, or the prime number has a token on it, lose a turn.
4. The first team to get three tokens in a row wins the game.
5. Play 3 games. The team winning 2 out of 3 games wins.

7	**13**	**29**
2	**11**	**5**
3	**23**	**19**

Die × Die + or –1 Prime Number

Four-Grid Tic-Tac-Toe

- Each team tosses a die.
- Higher number goes first.
- Each team chooses a color token.

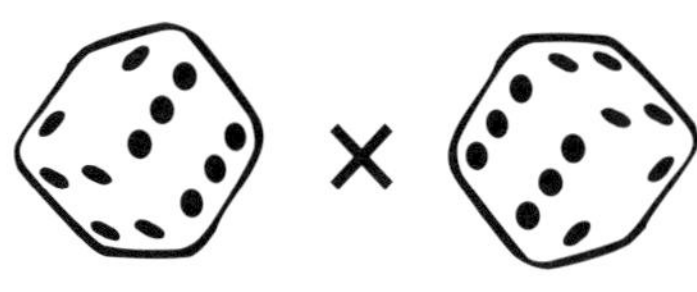

How to Play

1. *Toss 2 dice. Find the product. Either add 1 to the product or subtract 1 from the product.*
2. *If that number is a prime number, find it on any of the Tic-Tac-Toe grids and place a token on it.*
3. *If the number is not a prime number, or if the prime number is not available on any grid, lose a turn.*
4. *The team with the most "three tokens in a row" wins.*

11	13	23	17	5	7
5	7	19	19	11	13
13	3	11	31	2	5
3	7	5	5	11	29
11	13	17	23	5	19
2	19	37	11	3	7

One-Die Factorial (!) Tic-Tac-Toe

- Each team tosses a die.
- Higher number goes first.
- Each team chooses a color token.

How to Play

1. Toss a die.

2. Place a token on the factorial of the number tossed.

1! = 1 *2! = 2 × 1* *3! = 3 × 2 × 1*

4! = 4 × 3 × 2 × 1 *5! = 5 × 4 × 3 × 2 × 1* *6! = 6 × 5 × 4 × 3 × 2 × 1*

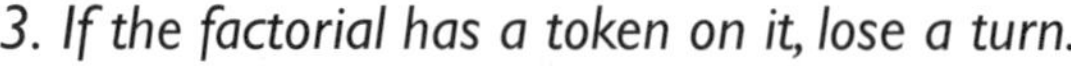

3. If the factorial has a token on it, lose a turn.

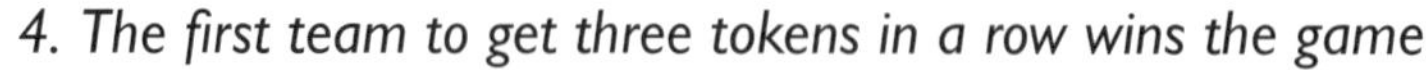

4. The first team to get three tokens in a row wins the game.

5. Play 3 games. The team winning 2 out of 3 games wins.

720	**120**	**24**
2	**6**	**2**
120	**24**	**1**

Four-Grid Tic-Tac-Toe

One-Die Factorial (!)

- Each team tosses a die.
- Higher number goes first.
- Each team chooses a color token.

How to Play

1. *Toss a die.*
2. *Place a token on the factorial of the number tossed.*

   1! = 1 *2! = 2 × 1* *3! = 3 × 2 × 1*

   4! = 4 × 3 × 2 × 1 *5! = 5 × 4 × 3 × 2 × 1* *6! = 6 × 5 × 4 × 3 × 2 × 1*
3. *If the factorial is not available on any grid, lose a turn.*
4. *The team with the most "three tokens in a row" wins.*

24	120	1	720	2	6
120	2	720	6	24	1
6	1	24	720	1	120
6	720	2	6	120	2
2	120	24	24	720	1
720	1	6	120	2	24

Tic-Tac-Toe

One-Die Summation (Σ)

- Each team tosses a die.
- Higher number goes first.
- Each team chooses a color token.

How to Play

1. *Toss a die. Place a token on the* ***summation (Σ)*** *of the number tossed.*

   $\Sigma 1 = 1$ $\Sigma 2 = 2 + 1$ $\Sigma 3 = 3 + 2 + 1$

   $\Sigma 4 = 4 + 3 + 2 + 1$ $\Sigma 5 = 5 + 4 + 3 + 2 + 1$ $\Sigma 6 = 6 + 5 + 4 + 3 + 2 + 1$
2. *If the* ***summation*** *is already taken, lose a turn.*
3. *The first team to get three tokens in a row wins.*
4. *Play 3 games. The team winning 2 out of 3 games wins.*

21	**15**	**10**
3	**6**	**3**
21	**10**	**1**

- Each team tosses a die.
- Higher number goes first.
- Each team chooses a color token.

Four-Grid Tic-Tac-Toe
One-Die Summation (Σ)

$\sum 1 = 1$

$\sum 2 = 2 + 1$

$\sum 3 = 3 + 2 + 1$

$\sum 4 = 4 + 3 + 2 + 1$

$\sum 5 = 5 + 4 + 3 + 2 + 1$

$\sum 6 = 6 + 5 + 4 + 3 + 2 + 1$

How to Play

1. *Toss a die.*
2. *Find the* ***summation (Σ)*** *of the number tossed on one of the Tic-Tac-Toe grids and place a token on it.*
3. *If the* ***summation*** *is not available on any of the grids, lose a turn.*
4. *Team with the most "three tokens in a row" wins.*

10	15	1	21	3	6
15	3	21	6	10	1
6	1	10	21	1	15
6	21	3	6	15	3
3	21	10	10	21	1
21	1	6	15	3	10

Two-Dice Summation (Σ)

Tic-Tac-Toe

- Each team tosses a die.
- Higher number goes first.
- Each team chooses a color token.

How to Play

1. *Toss two dice. Find the sum.*
2. *Place a token on the* ***summation (Σ)*** *of the sum. For example,*
   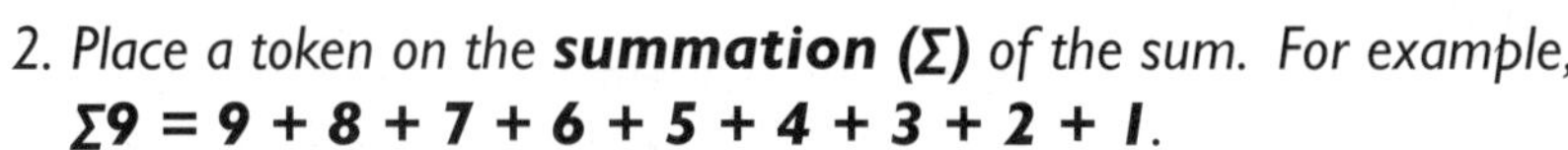
   Σ9 = 9 + 8 + 7 + 6 + 5 + 4 + 3 + 2 + 1*.*
3. *If the* ***summation*** *is already taken, lose a turn.*
4. *The first team to get three tokens in a row wins the game.*
5. *Play 3 games. The team winning 2 out of 3 games wins.*

21	**15**	**66**
36	**28**	**6**
55	**10**	**45**

Four-Grid Tic-Tac-Toe

Two-Dice Summation (Σ)

- Each team tosses a die.
- Higher number goes first.
- Each team chooses a color token.

How to Play

1. *Toss two dice. Find the sum of the two dice.*
2. *Place a token on the* ***summation (Σ)*** *of the sum. For example,* $\Sigma 9 = 9 + 8 + 7 + 6 + 5 + 4 + 3 + 2 + 1$.
3. *If the number is already taken, lose a turn.*
4. *Team with the most "three tokens in a row" wins.*

28	21	36	55	36	66
55	15	10	15	28	45
45	21	6	10	36	21
10	45	6	66	28	15
21	36	78	55	21	28
28	15	28	36	45	3

Positive and Negative Numbers

Tic-Tac-Toe

- Each team tosses a die.
- Higher number goes first.
- Each team chooses a color token.

How to Play

1. Toss a green die and a red die. Compute the sum or difference.
Example: green die = 3, red die = –5. Compute: (+3) + (–5) = –2.

2. Place a token on the number.

3. If the number is not available, lose a turn.

4. First team to get three tokens in a row wins the game.

5. Play 3 games. Team winning 2 out of 3 games wins.

–2	**+1**	**–3**
+3	**0**	**+2**
–4	**+5**	**–1**

Positive and Negative Numbers

Four-Grid Tic-Tac-Toe

- Each team tosses a die.
- Higher number goes first.
- Each team chooses a color token.

How to Play

1. *Toss a green die and a red die. Compute the sum or difference. Example: green die = 3, red die = –5. Compute: (+3) + (–5) = –2.*
2. *Find the number on any of the Tic-Tac-Toe grids and place a token on it.*
3. *If the number is not available on any grid, lose a turn.*
4. *Team with the most "three tokens in a row" wins.*

–3	+1	–2	0	+2	–5
+4	+2	+1	–4	+1	–1
–1	+3	0	–3	–2	+3
+3	0	+1	–1	+1	–3
–2	–1	–3	+3	0	+2
–4	+5	+2	–2	+4	–1

Aim For Activities

Contents

Directions for Aim For Activities

Objectives

- Develop a working knowledge of the mathematical concept of adding positive and negative integers 1 through 6.
- Practice computing the sum of positive and negative integers 1 through 6.

Toss	Team A	Team B
1		
2		
3		
4		
5		
Total		

Introduce the **Aim For** activities by demonstrating on an overhead and playing against the class.

Two teams on a team are suggested. Teams give students an opportunity to discuss moves and strategies and provide a check on correct computation.

How to Play

Green dice = positive numbers

Red dice = negative numbers

- Each team tosses a die. Higher number goes first.
- A team member tosses all twelve dice, 6 green and 6 red
- Teams take turns selecting a die from the group of 12 dice, aiming for a score of 0, –1, +1, –2, or +2, (depending on the activity) after selecting 6 dice.
- Teams tally their 6 dice selections and record the total on the chart.
- After 5 tosses, teams tally all 5 scores to determine the winner.

Suggestions

- Before teams tally their score, encourage them to predict which team will win.
- After 3 or 4 tosses, teams calculate what they need to aim for in the next toss or 2 tosses to win.

Variations

- Add more tosses—10, 15, or more.
- Add more dice.

Discussion

- Is this more a game of luck or skill?
- Would adding more dice to the activity influence the outcome? Would it make it more or less a game of luck or skill? Explain.
- Would adding more tosses to the activity influence the outcome? Would it make it more or less a game of luck or skill? Explain.
- Would adding more teams to the activity influence the outcome? Explain.

Aim for Zero

- Each team tosses a die.
- Higher number goes first.

Green Dice = Positive Numbers 1, 2, 3, 4, 5, 6
Red Dice = Negative Numbers –1, –2, –3, –4, –5, –6

How to Play

1. A team member tosses all 12 dice—6 green dice and 6 red dice.
2. Teams take turns selecting one green die and one red die from the 12 dice tossed, aiming for a score of 0 after selecting 6 dice.
3. Teams tally their 6 dice and record the sum on the chart.
4. After 5 tosses, teams tally their scores. Team whose score is closest to zero wins.

Toss	Team A	Team B
1		
2		
3		
4		
5		
Total		

Aim for Negative One

- Each team tosses a die.
- Higher number goes first.

Green Dice = Positive Numbers 1, 2, 3, 4, 5, 6
Red Dice = Negative Numbers –1, –2, –3, –4, –5, –6

How to Play

1. *A team member tosses all 12 dice—6 green dice and 6 red dice.*
2. *Teams take turns selecting one green die and one red die from the 12 dice tossed, aiming for a score of –1 after selecting 6 dice.*
3. *Teams tally their 6 dice and record the sum on the chart.*
4. *After 5 tosses, teams tally their scores. Team whose score is closest to –1 wins.*

Toss	Team A	Team B
1		
2		
3		
4		
5		
Total		

Aim for Positive One

- Each team tosses a die.
- Higher number goes first.

Green Dice = Positive Numbers 1, 2, 3, 4, 5, 6
Red Dice = Negative Numbers –1, –2, –3, –4, –5, –6

How to Play

1. A team member tosses all 12 dice—6 green dice and 6 red dice.

2. Teams take turns selecting one green die and one red die from the 12 dice tossed, aiming for a score of +1 after selecting 6 dice.

3. Teams tally their 6 dice and record the sum on the chart.

4. After 5 tosses, teams tally their scores. Team whose score is closest to +1 wins.

Toss	Team A	Team B
1		
2		
3		
4		
5		
Total		

Aim For Negative Two

- Each team tosses a die.
- Higher number goes first.

Green Dice = Positive Numbers 1, 2, 3, 4, 5, 6
Red Dice = Negative Numbers –1, –2, –3, –4, –5, –6

How to Play

1. A team member tosses all 12 dice—6 green dice and 6 red dice.
2. Teams take turns selecting one green die and one red die from the 12 dice tossed, aiming for a score of –2 after selecting 6 dice.
3. Teams tally their 6 dice and record the sum on the chart.
4. After 5 tosses, teams tally their scores. Team whose score is closest to –2 wins.

Toss	Team A	Team B
1		
2		
3		
4		
5		
Total		

Aim For Positive Two

- Each team tosses a die.
- Higher number goes first.

Green Dice = Positive Numbers 1, 2, 3, 4, 5, 6
Red Dice = Negative Numbers –1, –2, –3, –4, –5, –6

How to Play

1. A team member tosses all 12 dice—6 green dice and 6 red dice.

2. Teams take turns selecting one green die and one red die from the 12 dice tossed, aiming for a score of +2 after selecting 6 dice.

3. Teams tally their 6 dice and record the sum on the chart.

4. After 5 tosses, teams tally their scores. Team whose score is closest to +2 wins.

Toss	Team A	Team B
1		
2		
3		
4		
5		
Total		

Independent Exploration Activities

Contents

Introduction to Independent Exploration Activities

Major published mathematical programs are research-based and attempt to achieve the goals of the NCTM standards. Most statewide assessment tests are based on students' thinking and the ability to express that thinking, rather than mastery of rules and procedures.

To ensure that some students are not left behind, all students must be provided with a menu of mathematics that is exciting and inviting. Not all students operate at the same level of proficiency; not all students have the same intellectual capacity. But all students can think, become problem solvers, and know how to work in teams to solve the problems of the workplace and their environment. While mastery of basic computation and number facts is important, mastery should not take precedence in developing mathematical thinkers. Students will not be employed based upon their ability to compute or demonstrate knowledge of the times tables. The ability to solve problems, think rationally, devise strategies, and collaborate in team approaches to solutions are traits that lead to success in the workplace.

Once students are familiar with the concepts of square numbers, square roots, prime numbers, positive and negative integers, factorials, and summations, as explored in the preceding activities, they are ready to apply this knowledge in generating math equations using a random set of numbers. The activities that follow are varied and offer only a sample of what is possible. Many can be modified and extended to provide for differentiated learning styles. Some of the activities continue to employ the use of dice. One such activity invites a team of students to toss seven dice and attempt to construct as many equations as possible. A modified version of this activity limits the students to using the seven dice to find solutions that equal the numbers 1 through 5.

There are classic challenges found in a variety of source materials that may not use dice. For example, "Using three 3s, write equations that equal the numbers 1 through 10," or "Using four 4s, write the numbers 1 through 100." The teacher can modify the second challenge to finding solutions 1 through 10. Once the students are engaged and interested in the activity, expand it to include the numbers 11 through 20.

Still other activities can challenge the students to use the numbers 1, 2, 3, 4, and 5 to create equations that equal the numbers 1 through 10. A favorite is to use just two 4s to write as many equations as possible. Initially, students of any age might think only of the obvious equations: $4 + 4 = 8$, $4 - 4 = 0$, $4 \times 4 = 16$, and $4 \div 4 = 1$. But once the door of mathematical creativity has been opened, they will find that there are well over 25 equations involving just 4s. Consider, for example, $\sqrt{4} \times \sum 4$—the square root of 4 times four summation, or 2×10, which equals 20. A slight reversal of the numbers and you could produce four summation (10) to the second power, yielding 100. These activities are an opportunity for the teacher to think outside the box of following mathematical rules and, instead, focus on employing mathematical reasoning.

The focus of *Dice Activities for Mathematical Thinking* is to provide a means for students to develop mathematical thinking skills by stimulating curiosity about and a passion for math, deepening their knowledge base, and encouraging playing with mathematical ideas. The activities are not meant to be used as "typical" worksheets, or graded as such. Rather, they are meant to be works in progress. A "work" sheet is a place for students to record their thinking, modify their predictions, and correct their errors, and not a means for judging their outcomes. Most importantly, the teacher should take note of the students' thinking and increased knowledge and skills, rather than judge on the basis of how many right or how many wrong. The constant judging/grading of every piece of work diminishes intrinsic motivation, shifting it to extrinsic motivation. The classroom should be considered a place of daily learning rather than a daily gauntlet to be maneuvered by the child.

Encourage small groups of students to work together, creating a learning environment where students have opportunities to share their thinking, ask for clarification, think about the mathematics, and not necessarily be driven to see how many "right" answers they can get. Explain to your class that this is their opportunity to actually learn the mathematics involved and that you will expect the same level of proficiency on a test or quiz.

Consider collaborating with colleagues at the same grade level. Decide on an activity

to be explored simultaneously, such as the **Summation (Σ) Toss Chart** (page 103). Create a friendly but competitive spirit among the different classrooms at a specific grade level and see which class can find all the answers first. Post a copy of the chart for the particular activity outside each classroom and check off the problems that have been solved. However, do not post the solutions, as this would deter the other classrooms from seeking a solution and inhibit additional creative thinking. The first class to solve all the problems would be declared the winner and then must prove their answers were correct. It is conceivable that the first "winner" might indeed not have all the correct solutions, and the competition would continue.

Consider opening one of the activities, such as **1, 2, 3, 4, 5 Square Number Chart** (page 107), to the entire grade as a homework assignment. More than likely this would generate energy and enthusiasm among the parent community as well as older siblings. Mathematical conversations and inquiries would compete with soccer scores as the main dinner table talk. Parents would see math as a subject that develops higher-level thinking, both inductive and deductive, rather than a continuous memorization of rules and procedures.

—The Authors

To the Student

Using Your Math Log

In the real world of problem solving, it often takes months or even years to find solutions, but mathematicians use their notes to reflect on their attempts and see if they provide clues to the eventual solution to a problem.

Save your work. Do not erase or cross out wrong answers. They just might provide a clue that will help you and your partners solve the problem. Some of the "almost" solutions may be useful as stepping-stones to generating other equations.

Make sure you state the problem you are working on so you can easily keep your records straight. Use both sides of the paper.

Generating Equations – Getting Started

Before generating equations, look at the numbers on the tossed dice. Ask yourself:

- What factorials are possible? (List them.)
- What summations are possible? (List them.)
- Are there any square numbers or combinations of numbers that will produce a square number?
- If "2" isn't available to use as an exponent, is there a combination of numbers that will equal 2 (for example, 5^{3-1})?
- Is there a combination that will equal 0? If so, what happens to a number when its exponent is 0?

For the purposes of these exercises, you can combine two numbers to make a double or triple-digit number. For example, a 2 and a 5 can be combined to make 25, or a 1, 1, and 2 can be combined to make 121. Make a list of the numbers you can make using this method.

Make a list of possible square roots or square numbers—for example, $\sqrt{(\Sigma 5)} + 1$ or $(\Sigma 4)^{\sqrt{4}}$.

Will any of the numbers produce a fraction or a decimal that equals $\frac{1}{2}$?

Finally, remember the PEMDAS rule. Use parenthesis and brackets to show which operations to perform first to make your equation true.

MATH LOG

Name: ______________________ Team Members: ______________________

Date: ______________________ ______________________

State the problem:

Attempts to solve the problem:

(When you have found a solution, circle it and copy it to the chart you're working on.)

Directions for Independent Explorations

Using a Random Set of Numbers

Objectives

- To generate equations using a random set of numbers
- To employ mathematical reasoning
- To deepen the knowledge base of the mathematical concepts of
  - Square numbers
  - Square roots
  - Prime numbers
  - Positive/negative integers
  - Factorials
  - Summation
- To gain an appreciation and working knowledge of order of operations

Activities

- **1 through 25 Toss**
- **Square Number Toss**
- **Prime Number Toss**
- **Summation Toss**

Introduce by demonstrating on an overhead and working with the **Getting Started** activity (page 96) to prepare students for generating number sentences for each chart.

Teams of 2, 3, or 4 students are suggested. Teams give students an opportunity to share their thinking, ask for clarification, and provide a check on correct computation.

How to Play

- Teacher tosses 5 dice.
- Teams use the **Getting Started** activity to focus their thinking. Each student keeps a complete record of his or her work.
- Using all five numbers, students generate equations that equal the numbers given on the chart.
- Students write equations in the appropriate box on the chart.
- The class works collaboratively to arrive at equations for each number on the chart.
- The teacher again tosses 5 dice. Students, working in small groups, use the **Getting Started** activity to focus on the new set of 5 numbers.
- Students generate equations that equal the numbers given on the chart.

Options

- Activity as a teaching tool – Groups give each other hints about how to form an equation for a particular number. Students share equations, seeing how many variations they can find for each number.
- Activity as a competition within the class – The group that finds the most solutions wins.
- Activity as a friendly competition among classes at the same grade level. Post a chart outside each classroom. Students check off problems that have been solved but do not post solutions, spurring on others to find solutions.

Suggestions

- Use 6 or 7 dice to differentiate learning by making activities less challenging. Using more dice provides more options for generating equations. Students can try using all 6 or 7 dice to generate an equation or choose which 5 numbers they want to use.
- Use just 4 dice to differentiate learning by making activities more challenging. Extend the 0–25 activity to 100.

Variations

- Team tosses a specified number of dice and writes as many equations as possible. Team tosses dice again and attempts to fill in missing equations. Students use a different-colored pencil to record equations generated by the second dice toss. Students continue tossing dice, recording new equations in a different color until the chart is complete.
- Team tosses dice and generates an equation for the first number on the chart. Team tosses dice again, writing an equation for the next number in sequence on the chart. Team continues tossing dice and writing equations for each number on the chart.
- Use as a competition between two teams. Team 1 tosses dice and generates an equation. Team 2 tosses dice and generates an equation. If a team cannot generate an equation from the toss, the team loses a turn. Numbers must be filled in sequence.
- Extend the activities tossing 7, 6, 5, or 4 dice by finding as many equations as possible that equal solutions 0 through 100 or even higher.
- Tossing 7, 6, 5, or 4 dice, generate as many solutions as possible for equations equaling 0 through 5 or 0 through 10.

Toss Chart (0–25)

How to Play

1. Toss 5 dice.
2. Using all 5 numbers, generate as many number equations that equal 0 through 25 as you can. Record the equations on the chart.
3. Toss the dice again to see if you can complete the chart.
4. Record the equations from the second toss using a different-colored pen or pencil.
5. See if you can complete the chart with just 3 tosses.

* Challenge: See how many equations you can write through 100.

* Challenge: Use 4 dice.

* More options for generating equations: Use 6 or 7 dice.

0 =	**13 =**
1 =	**14 =**
2 =	**15 =**
3 =	**16 =**
4 =	**17 =**
5 =	**18 =**
6 =	**19 =**
7 =	**20 =**
8 =	**21 =**
9 =	**22 =**
10 =	**23 =**
11 =	**24 =**
12 =	**25 =**

Square Number Toss Chart

How to Play

1. *Toss 5 dice.*
2. *Using all 5 numbers, generate as many equations as you can from the toss. Record the equations on the chart.*
3. *Toss the dice again to see if you can complete the chart.*
4. *Record the equations from the second toss using a different-colored pen or pencil.*
5. *See if you can complete the chart with less than 3 tosses.*

* *Challenge: Use 4 dice.*

* *More options for generating equations: Use 6 or 7 dice.*

1 =
4 =
9 =
16 =
25 =
36 =
49 =
64 =
81 =
100 =
121 =
144 =

Prime Number Toss Chart

How to Play

1. Toss 5 dice.

2. Using all 5 numbers, generate as many prime number equations as you can from the toss. Record the equations on the chart.

3. Toss the dice again to see if you can complete the chart.

4. Record the equations from the second toss using a different-colored pen or pencil.

5. See if you can complete the chart with just 3 tosses.

** Challenge: Use 4 dice.*

** More options for generating equations: Use 6 or 7 dice.*

2 =	**43 =**
3 =	**47 =**
5 =	**53 =**
7 =	**59 =**
11 =	**61 =**
13 =	**67 =**
17 =	**71 =**
19 =	**73 =**
23 =	**79 =**
29 =	**83 =**
31 =	**89 =**
37 =	**97 =**
41 =	**101 =**

Summation (Σ) Toss Chart

How to Play

1. *Toss 5 dice.*
2. *Using all 5 numbers, generate as many summation equations as you can from the toss. Record the equations on the chart.*
3. *Toss the dice again to see if you can complete the chart.*
4. *Record the equations from the second toss using a different-colored pen or pencil.*
5. *See if you can complete the chart with just 3 tosses.*

* *Challenge: Use 4 dice.*

* *More options for generating equations: Use 6 or 7 dice.*

Σ1 = 1 =
Σ2 = 3 =
Σ3 = 6 =
Σ4 = 10 =
Σ5 = 15 =
Σ6 = 21 =
Σ7 = 28 =
Σ8 = 36 =
Σ9 = 45 =
Σ10 = 55 =
Σ11 = 66 =
Σ12 = 78 =

Directions for Independent Explorations

Using a Specific Set of Numbers

Objectives

- To generate equations using a specific set of numbers
- To employ mathematical reasoning
- To deepen the knowledge base of the mathematical concepts of
  - Square numbers
  - Square roots
  - Prime numbers
  - Positive/negative integers
  - Factorials
  - Summation
- To gain an appreciation and working knowledge of order of operations

Activities

- **1, 2, 3, 4, 5**
- **Four 4s**
- **Five 5s**
- **Three 3s**
- **Two 4s**

Introduce by demonstrating on an overhead and working with the Getting Started activity (page 96) to prepare students for generating number sentences for each chart.

Teams of 2, 3, or 4 students are suggested. Teams give students an opportunity to share their thinking, ask for clarification, and provide a check on correct computation.

How to Play

- Using a set of specified numbers—three 3s, two 4s, four 4s, five 5s, or the numbers 1, 2, 3, 4, 5—students use the Getting Started activity to focus their thinking on generating equations that equal the numbers 0 through 25. Each student keeps a record of all his or her work.
- Students write equations in the appropriate box on the chart.
- The class works collaboratively to arrive at equations for each number on the chart using specific numbers: three 3s, two 4s, four 4s, five 5s, or the numbers 1, 2, 3, 4, or 5.
- Students, working in small groups, generate equations that equal the numbers 0 through 25, or 50, or 100.

Options

- Activity as a teaching tool – Groups give each other hints about how to form an equation for a particular number. Students share equations, seeing how many variations they can find for each number.
- Activity as a competition within the class – The group that finds the most solutions wins.
- Activity as a friendly competition among classes at the same grade level. Post a chart outside each classroom. Students check off problems that have been solved but do not post solutions, spurring on others to find solutions.

Suggestions

- To differentiate learning, limit or expand the number of equations. Some groups might generate equations for the first 10 numbers, while others might be encouraged to generate 2 equations for each number.
- Consider giving one of the activities (such as 1, 2, 3, 4, 5) to the grade level as a homework assignment, encouraging parents and siblings to participate.

Variations

- Using specific numbers, students generate equations for the Square Number Chart, the Prime Number Chart, and the Summation Chart.
- Extend the activities tossing 7, 6, 5, or 4 dice, or using three 3s, four 4s, and five 5s to find as many equations as possible equaling solutions 0 through 100 or even higher.
- Generate as many equations as possible tossing 7, 6, 5, or 4 dice, or using three 3s, four 4s, and five 5s for each solution 0 through 5 or 0 through 10.

1, 2, 3, 4, 5 Zero through 25 Chart

How to Play

Using the numbers 1, 2, 3, 4, and 5 only ONCE each, generate an equation that equals each number, 0 through 25.

** Challenge: See how many equations you can write that equal 26 through 100.*

0 =	**13 =**
1 =	**14 =**
2 =	**15 =**
3 =	**16 =**
4 =	**17 =**
5 =	**18 =**
6 =	**19 =**
7 =	**20 =**
8 =	**21 =**
9 =	**22 =**
10 =	**23 =**
11 =	**24 =**
12 =	**25 =**

1, 2, 3, 4, 5 Square Number Chart

How to Play

Using the numbers 1, 2, 3, 4, and 5 only ONCE each, generate an equation that equals each square number on the chart.

1 =
4 =
9 =
16 =
25 =
36 =
49 =
64 =
81 =
100 =
121 =
144 =

1, 2, 3, 4, 5 Prime Number Chart

How to Play

Using the numbers 1, 2, 3, 4, and 5 only ONCE each, generate an equation that equals each prime number on the chart.

2 =	**43 =**
3 =	**47 =**
5 =	**53 =**
7 =	**59 =**
11 =	**61 =**
13 =	**67 =**
17 =	**71 =**
19 =	**73 =**
23 =	**79 =**
29 =	**83 =**
31 =	**89 =**
37 =	**97 =**
41 =	**101 =**

1, 2, 3, 4, 5 Summation (Σ) Chart

How to Play

Using the numbers 1, 2, 3, 4, and 5 only ONCE each, generate an equation that equals each summation number on the chart.

$\Sigma 1 = 1 =$
$\Sigma 2 = 3 =$
$\Sigma 3 = 6 =$
$\Sigma 4 = 10 =$
$\Sigma 5 = 15 =$
$\Sigma 6 = 21 =$
$\Sigma 7 = 28 =$
$\Sigma 8 = 36 =$
$\Sigma 9 = 45 =$
$\Sigma 10 = 55 =$
$\Sigma 11 = 66 =$
$\Sigma 12 = 78 =$

4, 4, 4, 4 Zero through 25 Chart

How to Play

Using four 4s, generate an equation that equals each number, 0 through 25.

** Challenge: See how many equations you can write that equal 26 through 100.*

0 =	**13 =**
1 =	**14 =**
2 =	**15 =**
3 =	**16 =**
4 =	**17 =**
5 =	**18 =**
6 =	**19 =**
7 =	**20 =**
8 =	**21 =**
9 =	**22 =**
10 =	**23 =**
11 =	**24 =**
12 =	**25 =**

4, 4, 4, 4 Square Number Chart

How to Play

Using four 4s, generate an equation that equals each square number on the chart.

1 =
4 =
9 =
16 =
25 =
36 =
49 =
64 =
81 =
100 =
121 =
144 =

4, 4, 4, 4 Prime Number Chart

How to Play

Using four 4s, generate an equation that equals each prime number on the chart.

2 =	**43 =**
3 =	**47 =**
5 =	**53 =**
7 =	**59 =**
11 =	**61 =**
13 =	**67 =**
17 =	**71 =**
19 =	**73 =**
23 =	**79 =**
29 =	**83 =**
31 =	**89 =**
37 =	**97 =**
41 =	**101 =**

4, 4, 4, 4 Summation (Σ) Chart

How to Play

Using four 4s, generate an equation that equals each summation number on the chart.

Σ1 = 1 =
Σ2 = 3 =
Σ3 = 6 =
Σ4 = 10 =
Σ5 = 15 =
Σ6 = 21 =
Σ7 = 28 =
Σ8 = 36 =
Σ9 = 45 =
Σ10 = 55 =
Σ11 = 66 =
Σ12 = 78 =

5, 5, 5, 5, 5 Zero through 25 Chart

How to Play

Using five 5s, generate an equation that equals each number, 0 through 25.

** Challenge: See how many equations you can write that equal 26 through 100.*

0 =	**13 =**
1 =	**14 =**
2 =	**15 =**
3 =	**16 =**
4 =	**17 =**
5 =	**18 =**
6 =	**19 =**
7 =	**20 =**
8 =	**21 =**
9 =	**22 =**
10 =	**23 =**
11 =	**24 =**
12 =	**25 =**

5, 5, 5, 5, 5 Square Number Chart

How to Play

Using five 5s, generate an equation that equals each square number on the chart.

1 =
4 =
9 =
16 =
25 =
36 =
49 =
64 =
81 =
100 =
121 =
144 =

5, 5, 5, 5, 5 Prime Number Chart

How to Play

Using five 5s, generate an equation that equals each prime number on the chart.

2 =	**43 =**
3 =	**47 =**
5 =	**53 =**
7 =	**59 =**
11 =	**61 =**
13 =	**67 =**
17 =	**71 =**
19 =	**73 =**
23 =	**79 =**
29 =	**83 =**
31 =	**89 =**
37 =	**97 =**
41 =	**101 =**

5, 5, 5, 5, 5 Summation (Σ) Chart

How to Play

Using five 5s, generate an equation that equals each summation number on the chart.

Σ1 = 1 =
Σ2 = 3 =
Σ3 = 6 =
Σ4 = 10 =
Σ5 = 15 =
Σ6 = 21 =
Σ7 = 28 =
Σ8 = 36 =
Σ9 = 45 =
Σ10 = 55 =
Σ11 = 66 =
Σ12 = 78 =

3, 3, 3 Zero through 25 Chart

How to Play

Using three 3s, generate an equation that equals each number, 0 through 25.

** Challenge: See how many equations you can write that equal 26 through 100.*

0 =	13 =
1 =	14 =
2 =	15 =
3 =	16 =
4 =	17 =
5 =	18 =
6 =	19 =
7 =	20 =
8 =	21 =
9 =	22 =
10 =	23 =
11 =	24 =
12 =	25 =

4, 4 Zero through 25 Chart

How to Play

Using just two 4s, generate an equation that equals each number, 0 through 25.

** Challenge: See how many equations you can write that equal 26 through 100.*

0 =	**13 =**
1 =	**14 =**
2 =	**15 =**
3 =	**16 =**
4 =	**17 =**
5 =	**18 =**
6 =	**19 =**
7 =	**20 =**
8 =	**21 =**
9 =	**22 =**
10 =	**23 =**
11 =	**24 =**
12 =	**25 =**

Possible Solutions

Page 106

1, 2, 3, 4, 5 Zero Through 25 Chart

$0 = [(5 - 4) - (3 - 2)] \times 1$	$13 = 4^2 - (\sqrt{5 + 3 + 1})$
$1 = [(5 - 4) \times (3 - 2)] \times 1$	$14 = (5 \times 2) + [\Sigma 4 - (\Sigma 3 \times 1)]$
$2 = [\Sigma 4 - 5) \div (3 + 2)] + 1$	$15 = (5 \times 2) + [\Sigma 4 - (\Sigma 3 - 1)]$
$3 = [(5^2 - 1) \div 4] - 3$	$16 = (25 - 13) + 4$
$4 = [(45 \div 3) \div \Sigma 2] - 1$	$17 = [(4! - \Sigma 5) + 3^2] - 1$
$5 = [\{(5 \times 4) + 1\} \div 3] - 2$	$18 = [(4! - \Sigma 5) + 3^2] \times 1$
$6 = (21 \div 3) - (5 - 4)$	$19 = 3^2 + (5 + 4 + 1)$
$7 = (21 \div 3) \times (5 - 4)$	$20 = [(5! \div 3) \times 2] \div 4^1$
$8 = (42 - 35) + 1$	$21 = 23 - [(5 - 4) + 1]$
$9 = (5^2 + \sqrt{4}) \div (3 \times 1)$	$22 = (54 - 32) \times 1$
$10 = (5 + 4 + 1) \times (3 - 2)$	$23 = 23 \times [(5 - 4) \times 1]$
$11 = [(\Sigma 4 \div 5) \times (2 \times 3)] - 1$	$24 = (31 - 25) \times 4$
$12 = (5^2 - 1) - (3 \times 4)$	$25 = 25 \times [(4 - 3) \times 1]$

Page 107

1, 2, 3, 4, 5 Square Number 25 Chart

$1 = (5 - 4)^3 \times (2 - 1)$
$4 = (24 \div 3) - (5 - 1)$
$9 = [54 \div (3 \times 2)] \times 1$
$16 = 2^5 - 4^{3 - 1}$
$25 = 34 - [(5 \times 2) - 1]$
$36 = [5! \div 3) - [(\sqrt{4} + 2) \times 1]$
$49 = 54 - (2 + 3)^1$
$64 = [(4 \times 2) \times (5 + 3)] \times 1$
$81 = [3^2 \times (4 + 5)] \times 1$
$100 = 5! - [4^2 + (3 + 1)]$
$121 = [5 + (2 \times 3)] \times (\Sigma 4 + 1)$
$144 = [(\Sigma 5 - 3) \times (\Sigma 4 + 2)] \div 1$

Page 108

Page 1, 2, 3, 4, 5 Prime Number Chart

$2 = [(5 + 3) - (4 + 2)] \times 1$	$43 = 2^5 + [(4 \times 3) - 1]$
$3 = (5 + 3) - (4 + 2) + 1$	$47 = (\Sigma 4 \times 5) - [3 \times (2 - 1)]$
$5 = (\sqrt{5 + 4}) + (3 + 1) - 2$	$53 = \Sigma 4 \times 5 + [3 \times (2 - 1)]$
$7 = 3^2 - [(5 - 4) + 1]$	$59 = (5! \div 2) - (4 - 3^1)$
$11 = [(3! \times 2) - (5 - 4)] \times 1$	$61 = (15 \times 4) + (3 - 2)$
$13 = [(3! \times 2) + (5 - 4)] \times 1$	$67 = (5 + 3)^2 + (3 \times 1)$
$17 = [(3 \times 5) + (4 - 2)] \times 1$	$71 = 4^3 + (5^1 + 2)$
$19 = [(4 \times 5) - (3 - 2)] \times 1$	$73 = [\Sigma(\Sigma 4)] + \Sigma 5 + [3 \times (2 - 1)]$
$23 = (4 \times 5) + [3 \times (2 - 1)]$	$79 = [\Sigma(\Sigma 4)] + \Sigma 5 + [3^2 \times (2 - 1)]$
$29 = 5^2 + [(3! - \sqrt{4}) \times 1]$	$83 = (45 \times 2) - (3! + 1)$
$31 = 5^2 + [(3 + 4) - 1]$	$89 = (\Sigma 4)^2 - [\Sigma 5 - (1 + 3)]$
$37 = 4! + [(5 \times 2) + 3]$	$97 = (4 \times 5^2) - (3 \times 1)$
$41 = 41 - [5 - (3 + 2)]$	$101 = (54 \times 2) - (3! + 1)$

Page 109

1, 2, 3, 4, 5 Summation (Σ) Chart

$\Sigma 1 = 1 = (34 - 2^5) - 1$
$\Sigma 2 = 3 = [24 \div (5 = 3)] \times 1$
$\Sigma 3 = 6 = (24 - 13) - 5$
$\Sigma 4 = 10 = (43 - 2^5) - 1$
$\Sigma 5 = 15 = (45 \div 3) \times (2 - 1)$
$\Sigma 6 = 21 = 4^2 + [\{\Sigma (3 + 1)\} - 5]$
$\Sigma 7 = 28 = (4 \times 3 \times 2) + (5 - 1)$
$\Sigma 8 = 36 = (15 + 23) - \sqrt{4}$
$\Sigma 9 = 45 = [\Sigma (5 \times 2)] - [(\Sigma 3 + 4) \times 1]$
$\Sigma 10 = 55 = [(3^2 \times 5) + \Sigma 4] \times 1$
$\Sigma 11 = 66 = [(4 \times 2) + 3] \times (5 + 1)$
$\Sigma 12 = 78 = 5! - [43 - (2 - 1)]$

Possible Solutions

Page 110

4, 4, 4, 4 Zero Through 25 Chart

$0 = 4^{\sqrt{4}} - 4^{\sqrt{4}}$	$13 = [(\Sigma\sqrt{4}) \times 4] + (4 \div 4)$
$1 = (4 \div 4) \times (4 \div 4)$	$14 = [(\Sigma\sqrt{4}) \times 4] + (4 \div \sqrt{4})$
$2 = (4 \div 4) + (4 \div 4)$	$15 = [\Sigma 4 \times \sqrt{4}] - (\Sigma 4 \div \sqrt{4})$
$3 = (\sqrt{4} + \sqrt{4}) - (4 \div 4)$	$16 = 4^{\sqrt{4}} \times (4 \div 4)$
$4 = (\sqrt{4} + \sqrt{4}) \div (4 \div 4)$	$17 = 4^{\sqrt{4}} + (4 \div 4)$
$5 = (\sqrt{4} + \sqrt{4}) + (4 \div 4)$	$18 = 4^{\sqrt{4}} + (4 \div \sqrt{4})$
$6 = (4! - 4) \times (4 \div 4)$	$19 = [\Sigma 4 \times \sqrt{4}] - (4 \div 4)$
$7 = (4! - 4) + (4 \div 4)$	$20 = [\Sigma 4 \times \sqrt{4}] \div (4 \div 4)$
$8 = (4! - 4) + (4 \div \sqrt{4})$	$21 = [\Sigma 4 \times \sqrt{4}] + (4 \div 4)$
$9 = (4 \times \sqrt{4}) + (4 \div 4)$	$22 = [\Sigma 4 \times \sqrt{4}] + (4 \div \sqrt{4})$
$10 = 4^{\sqrt{4}} - (\Sigma\sqrt{4})!$	$23 = 4! - [4 - (\Sigma\sqrt{4})]$
$11 = [(\Sigma\sqrt{4}) \times 4] - (4 \div 4)$	$24 = [\Sigma 4 \times \sqrt{4}] + (\sqrt{4} + \sqrt{4})$
$12 = [(\Sigma\sqrt{4}) \times 4] \times (4 \div 4)$	$25 = 4! + [4 - (\Sigma\sqrt{4})]$

Page 111

4, 4, 4, 4 Square Number Chart

$1 = (4 \div 4) \times (4 \div 4)$
$4 = (\sqrt{4} + \sqrt{4}) \times (4 \div 4)$
$9 = (4 + 4) + (4 \div 4)$
$16 = 4^{\sqrt{4}} \times (4 \div 4)$
$25 = [(\Sigma\sqrt{4})! \times 4] + (4 \div 4)$
$36 = [(\Sigma\sqrt{4})! \times (\Sigma\sqrt{4})!] \times (4 \div 4)$
$49 = 4! + 4! + (4 \div 4)$
$64 = 4^{4 - (4 \div 4)}$
$81 = [\Sigma 4 - (4 \div 4)]^{\sqrt{4}}$
$100 = (\Sigma 4 \times \Sigma 4) \times (4 \div 4)$
$121 = [\Sigma 4 + (4 \div 4)]^{\sqrt{4}}$
$144 = (4! \div \sqrt{4}) \times (4! \div \sqrt{4})$

Page 112

4, 4, 4, 4 Prime Number Chart

$2 = (4 \div 4) + (4 \div 4)$	$43 = [(\Sigma 4) \times 4] + [(\Sigma\sqrt{4})!) \div (\sqrt{4})]$
$3 = (\sqrt{4} + \sqrt{4}) - (4 \div 4)$	$47 = (4! + 4!) - (4 \div 4)$
$5 = (\sqrt{4} + \sqrt{4}) + (4 \div 4)$	$53 = (4! + 4!) + (\Sigma 4 \div \sqrt{4})$
$7 = (4 \times \sqrt{4}) - (4 \div 4)$	$59 = (4! \div .4) - (4 \div 4)$
$11 = (\Sigma\sqrt{4}) + [\Sigma 4 - (4 \div \sqrt{4})]$	$61 = (4! \div .4) + (4 \div 4)$
$13 = (\Sigma\sqrt{4} \times 4) + (4 \div 4)$	$67 = (4! \div .4) + [4 + \Sigma(\sqrt{4})]$
$17 = \Sigma\{4 + (4 \div 4)\} + \sqrt{4}$	$71 = [\Sigma(\Sigma 4) + \Sigma 4)] + (4 + \sqrt{4})$
$19 = \Sigma\{4 + (4 \div 4)\} + 4$	$73 = \Sigma[(\Sigma\sqrt{4})!] + \Sigma[(\Sigma\sqrt{4})!] + \Sigma[(\Sigma\sqrt{4})!] + \Sigma 4$
$23 = 4! - [4 \div (\sqrt{4} + \sqrt{4})]$	$79 = [\Sigma(\Sigma 4) + 4!] + (4 - 4)$
$29 = 4! + [4 + (4 \div 4)]$	$83 = [\Sigma(\Sigma 4) + 4!] + (\sqrt{4} + \sqrt{4})$
$31 = [(\Sigma\sqrt{4})! \times (\Sigma\sqrt{4})!] - (\Sigma 4 \div \sqrt{4})$	$89 = [4! \times 4) - 4] - \Sigma\sqrt{4}$
$37 = \{(\Sigma\sqrt{4})! \times (\Sigma\sqrt{4})!\} + (4 \div 4)$	$97 = (4! \times 4) + (4 \div 4)$
$41 = [(\Sigma 4) \times 4] + (4 \div 4)$	$101 = (\Sigma 4 \times \Sigma 4) + (4 \div 4)$

Possible Solutions

Page 113

4, 4, 4, 4 Summation (Σ) Chart

$\Sigma 1 = 1 = (4 \div 4) \div (4 \div 4)$
$\Sigma 2 = 3 = 4! \div (4 + \sqrt{4} + \sqrt{4})$
$\Sigma 3 = 6 = (4! \div 4) \times (4 \div 4)$
$\Sigma 4 = 10 = (\Sigma 4 \div \sqrt{4}) + (\Sigma 4 \div \sqrt{4})$
$\Sigma 5 = 15 = 4^{\sqrt{4}} - (4 \div 4)$
$\Sigma 6 = 12 = \Sigma(\Sigma\sqrt{4}) \times \sqrt{4}$
$\Sigma 7 = 28 = 44 - 4^{\sqrt{4}}$
$\Sigma 8 = 36 = 44 - (4 + 4)$
$\Sigma 9 = 45 = \Sigma[(4 + 4) + (4 \div 4)]$ *or* $44 + (4 \div 4)$
$\Sigma 10 = 55 = \Sigma[(4 + 4 + 4) - \sqrt{4}]$
$\Sigma 11 = 66 = \Sigma(\Sigma 4) + \Sigma 4 + (4 \div 4)$
$\Sigma 12 = 78 = [\Sigma 4(4 + 4)] - \sqrt{4}$

Page 114

5, 5, 5, 5, 5 Zero through 25 Chart

$0 = (55 - 55)^{5}$	$13 = [5! + (5 + 5)] \div (5 + 5)$
$1 = [(5 + 5) \div 5] - (5 \div 5)$	$14 = (5 + 5 + 5) - (5 \div 5)$
$2 = [(5 + 5) \div 5] \times (5 \div 5)$	$15 = (5 + 5 + 5) \times (5 \div 5)$
$3 = [(5 + 5) \div 5] + (5 \div 5)$	$16 = (5 \div .5) + [5 + (5 \div 5)]$
$4 = (5! \div 5) \div [5 + (5 \div 5)]$	$17 = (5 \times 5) - [5 + (\Sigma 5 \div 5)]$
$5 = (5 \div 5) \times (5 \div 5) \times 5$	$18 = [\Sigma 5 + (\Sigma 5 \div 5)] \times (5 \div 5)$
$6 = [(5 \div 5) \times (5 \div 5)] + 5$	$19 = (5! \div 5) - [5 \times (5 \div 5)]$
$7 = [(5 \div 5) + (5 \div 5)] + 5$	$20 = (5! \div 5) - [5 - (5 \div 5)]$
$8 = [(5 \times 5) \div 5] + (\Sigma 5 \div 5)$	$21 = [\Sigma 5 + \Sigma(\Sigma 5 \div 5)] \times (5 \div 5)$
$9 = [55 - (5 + 5)] \div 5$	$22 = (5! \div 5) - [5 - (\Sigma 5 \div 5)]$
$10 = (55 \div 5) - (5 \div 5)$	$23 = (5 \times 5) - [(5 + 5) \div 5]$
$11 = (55 \div 5) \div (5 \div 5)$	$24 = (\Sigma 5 - 5) + [5 - (5 \div 5)]$
$12 = (55 \div 5) + (5 \div 5)$	$25 = 55 - (5 \times 5) - 5$

Page 115

5, 5, 5, 5, 5 Square Number Chart

$1 = 5 \div [.5(5) + .5(5)]$
$4 = 5 - [(5 \div 5) \times (5 \div 5)]$
$9 = (\sqrt{5 \times 5}) + [5 - (5 \div 5)]$
$16 = \Sigma 5 + [(5 \div 5) \times (5 \div 5)]$
$25 = (\Sigma 5 + 5) + [5 \times (5 \div 5)]$
$36 = (\Sigma 5 + \Sigma 5) + [5 + (5 \div 5)]$
$49 = 5(5 + 5) - (5 \div 5)$
$64 = .5(5!) + [5 - (5 \div 5)]$
$81 = (\Sigma 5 \times 5) + [5 + (5 \div 5)]$
$100 = (5 \times 5) \times [5 - (5 \div 5)]$
$121 = 5! + [(5 \div 5) \times (5 \div 5)]$
$144 = 5! + [(5 \times 5) - (5 \div 5)]$

Page 116

5, 5, 5, 5, 5 Prime Number Chart

$2 = [(5 \div .5) \div 5] \div (5 \div 5)$	$43 = [5! \div (\Sigma 5 \div 5)] + (\Sigma 5 \div 5)$
$3 = [(5 \div .5) \div 5] + (5 \div 5)$	$47 = \Sigma(5 + 5) - [5 + (\Sigma 5 \div 5)]$
$5 = (\sqrt{5 \times 5} \div \sqrt{5 \times 5}) \times 5$	$53 = \Sigma(5 + 5) - [5 - (\Sigma 5 \div 5)]$
$7 = 5 + (5 \div 5) + (5 \div 5)$	$59 = .5(5!) - 5^{5-5}$
$11 = (\Sigma 5 \div 5) + 5 + (\Sigma 5 \div 5)$	$61 = .5(5!) + 5^{5-5}$
$13 = \Sigma 5 - [(5 \div 5) + (5 \div 5)]$	$67 = \Sigma(5 + 5) + .5(5! \div 5)$
$17 = \Sigma 5 + (5 \div 5) + (5 \div 5)$	$71 = 5(\Sigma 5) - [5 - (5 \div 5)]$
$19 = (5! \div 5) - [5 \times (5 \div 5)]$	$73 = 5(\Sigma 5) - [5 - (\Sigma 5 \div 5)]$
$23 = (5! \div 5) - 5^{5-5}$	$79 = 5(\Sigma 5) + 5 - (5 \div 5)$
$29 = (5! \div 5) + [5 \times (5 \div 5)]$	$83 = 5(\Sigma 5) + 5 + (\Sigma 5 \div 5)$
$31 = \Sigma 5 + \Sigma 5 + 5^{5-5}$	$89 = 5! - [(\Sigma 5 + \Sigma 5) + (5 \div 5)]$
$37 = 5 \times 5 + [\Sigma 5 - (\Sigma 5 \div 5)]$	$97 = 5! - (5! \div 5) + (5 \div 5)$
$41 = [5! \div (\Sigma 5 \div 5)] + (5 \div 5)$	$101 = 5! - \Sigma 5 - [5 - (5 \div 5)]$

Possible Solutions

Page 117

5, 5, 5, 5, 5 Summation (Σ) Chart

$\Sigma 1 = 1 = 5 \div [.5(5) + .5(5)]$
$\Sigma 2 = 3 = 5 - [(\Sigma 5 \div 5) - (5 \div 5)]$
$\Sigma 3 = 6 = [5 + (5 \div 5)] \times (5 \div 5)$
$\Sigma 4 = 10 = (\Sigma 5 + \Sigma 5 + \Sigma 5 + 5) \div 5$
$\Sigma 5 = 15 = (5 + 5 + 5) \div (5 \div 5)$
$\Sigma 6 = 21 = 5 \times 5 - [5 - (5 \div 5)]$
$\Sigma 7 = 28 = (5! \div 5) + [5 - (5 \div 5)]$
$\Sigma 8 = 36 = \Sigma[5 + (\Sigma 5 \div 5)] \times (5 \div 5)$
$\Sigma 9 = 45 = \Sigma(5 + 5) - \Sigma[5 - (5 \div 5)]$
$\Sigma 10 = 55 = 5 \times \Sigma[5 - (5 \div 5)] + 5$
$\Sigma 11 = 66 = 5! - \Sigma(5 + 5) + (5 \div 5)$
$\Sigma 12 = 78 = (\Sigma 5 \times 5) + (\Sigma 5 \div 5)$

Page 118

3, 3, 3 Zero through 25 Chart

$0 = (3 - 3) \times 3$	$13 = (3 \div .3) + 3$
$1 = 3 - (\Sigma 3 \div 3)$	$14 = (3! \div .3) - \Sigma 3$
$2 = 3 - (3 \div 3)$	$15 = (3 \times 3) + 3!$
$3 = (3 - 3) + 3$	$16 = (3 \div .3) + 3!$
$4 = (3 \div 3) + 3$	$17 = (3! \div .3) - 3$
$5 = 3! - (3 \div 3)$	$18 =$
$6 = 3! \times (3 \div 3)$	$19 =$
$7 = 3! + (3 \div 3)$	$20 =$
$8 = \Sigma 3 + (\Sigma 3 \div 3)$	$21 =$
$9 = 3 + 3 + 3$	$22 =$
$10 = \sqrt{3 \times 3} \div .3$	$23 =$
$11 = 33 \div 3$	$24 =$
$12 = 3! \times \Sigma 3 \div 3)$	$25 =$

Page 119

4, 4 Zero through 25 Chart

$0 = 4 - 4$	$13 = \Sigma 4 + \Sigma\sqrt{4}$
$1 = 4 \div 4$	$14 = \Sigma 4 + 4$
$2 = 4 - \sqrt{4}$	$15 = \Sigma[(\Sigma\sqrt{4})!] - (\Sigma\sqrt{4})!)$
$3 = (\Sigma\sqrt{4})! - \Sigma\sqrt{4}$	$16 = 4 \times 4$
$4 = \sqrt{4} + \sqrt{4}$	$17 = \Sigma[(\Sigma\sqrt{4})!] - 4$
$5 = \Sigma 4 \div \sqrt{4}$	$18 = \Sigma[(\Sigma\sqrt{4})!] - \Sigma\sqrt{4}$
$6 = 4! \div 4$	$19 = \Sigma[(\Sigma\sqrt{4})!] - \sqrt{4}$
$7 = \Sigma[(\Sigma\sqrt{4})!] \div \Sigma\sqrt{4}$	$20 = \Sigma 4 + \Sigma 4$
$8 = 4 + 4$	$21 = 4! - \Sigma\sqrt{4}$
$9 = (\Sigma\sqrt{4})! + \Sigma\sqrt{4}$	$22 = 4! - \sqrt{4}$
$10 = 4 \div .4$	$23 = \Sigma[(\Sigma\sqrt{4})!] + \sqrt{4}$
$11 = \Sigma(\Sigma\sqrt{4})! - \Sigma 4$	$24 = \Sigma[(\Sigma\sqrt{4})!] + \Sigma\sqrt{4}$
$12 = \Sigma 4 + \sqrt{4}$	$25 = \Sigma[(\Sigma\sqrt{4})!] + 4$

About the Authors

Mary Holt Saltus earned a CAS degree in human development from Harvard Graduate School of Education and a master's degree from Wheelock College. As a Peace Corps volunteer, she was a teacher trainer for the Van Leer Foundation for Early Childhood Education. Currently she is researching the link between understanding math concepts and reading comprehension.

Chet Delani holds a doctorate from Boston College and a master's degree in mathematics education from Boston University. A nationally recognized trainer of teachers in grades K–8 mathematics, he is a member of the faculty of Cambridge College in Cambridge, Massachusetts and has served on the faculties of Wheelock College, Boston College, and the University of Massachusetts/Boston. His work with classroom teachers is supported by 39 years as a classroom teacher and elementary school principal. Currently he is actively engaged in staff training in mathematics in school districts throughout Massachusetts.

Also by the same authors: *Dice Activities for Math* and *Dice Activities for Multiplication.* Available from Didax (www.didax.com/800-458-0024).